SAP® HANA – Implementation Guide

Bert Vanstechelman

Thank you for purchasing this book from Espresso Tutorials!

Like a cup of espresso coffee, Espresso Tutorials SAP books are concise and effective. We know that your time is valuable and we deliver information in a succinct and straightforward manner. It only takes our readers a short amount of time to consume SAP concepts. Our books are well recognized in the industry for leveraging tutorial-style instruction and videos to show you step by step how to successfully work with SAP.

Check out our YouTube channel to watch our videos at
https://www.youtube.com/user/EspressoTutorials.

If you are interested in SAP Finance and Controlling, join us at
http://www.fico-forum.com/forum2/
to get your SAP questions answered and contribute to discussions.

Related titles from Espresso Tutorials:

▶ Rob Frye, Joe Darlak, Dr. Bjarne Berg:
The SAP® BW to HANA Migration Handbook
http://5109.espresso-tutorials.com

▶ Dominique Alfermann, Stefan Hartmann, Benedikt Engel:
SAP® HANA Advanced Modeling
http://4110.espresso-tutorials.com

▶ Janet Salmon & Claus Wild:
First Steps in SAP® S/4HANA Finance:
http://5149.espresso-tutorials.com

▶ Frank Riesner, Klaus-Peter Sauer:
SAP® BW/4HANA and BW on HANA
http://5215.espresso-tutorials.com

Bert Vanstechelman
SAP® HANA – Implementation Guide

ISBN:	978-1-984181-42-8
Editor:	Karen Schoch
Cover Design:	Philip Esch, Martin Munzel
Cover Photo:	istockphoto.com #453516561 © Dant
Interior Book Design:	Johann-Christian Hanke

All rights reserved.

1st Edition 2018, Gleichen

© 2018 by Espresso Tutorials GmbH

URL: *www.espresso-tutorials.com*

Feedback
We greatly appreciate any kind of feedback you have concerning this book. Please mail us at *info@espresso-tutorials.com*.

Table of Contents

Introduction

SAP announced the end-of-support of all non-SAP HANA platforms by 2025. Part of this strategy is the release of new SAP components such as S4/HANA which is only available on the SAP HANA platform. As a result, more and more customers are considering or are already migrating to SAP HANA.

The purpose of this book is to assist system architects, technical consultants and IT managers with designing system architectures for the deployment of SAP applications on the SAP HANA system. Important topics such as production and non-production systems, deployment options, backup and recovery, data replication, high-availability and virtualization are discussed in detail.

The content is based on SAP product features up to July 2016 and includes the SAP HANA multitenant database containers and recent support for virtualization of production systems.

Content

Choosing a new hardware infrastructure for your critical business applications is never an easy task. Room for further growth, performance, and high-availability are just a few aspects which need to be taken into consideration. It is even more complicated with SAP HANA as it has many prerequisites for the hardware infrastructure. SAP HANA is only supported on certified hardware and needs to be deployed in a certain way to guarantee performance.

We start our adventure in Chapter 1 in which we talk about the SAP HANA technology, the editions, why it matters (the use cases) and the on-premise delivery options. We end the chapter with SAP HANA sizing, capacity planning guidelines and an introduction to data tiering.

The landscape layout discussion is continued in Chapter 2 in which we go into more detail about the on-premise deployment options and, because SAP HANA needs data, the data provisioning scenarios.

It is all about scalability in Chapter 3. What happens if you reach the physical capacity of your server? Luckily, there are scale-up and scale-out possibilities. The high-availability and data partitioning capabilities of scale-out are discussed as well.

Chapter 4 is on SAP HANA and disaster recovery. SAP HANA is an in-memory database. So what if the power fails? Fortunately, SAP HANA uses disk storage to provide a fallback in case of a system failure. Disk storage is usually not enough as it provides no point-in-time recovery possibilities. In this chapter, we discuss the SAP HANA database concepts and the different backup and recovery options of SAP HANA.

There are two disadvantages of the backup recovery procedure: first, the database can only be recovered up to the last log backup, and second, the application of log backups, especially when many exist, takes time because every entry in the log needs to be re-applied. A preferred solution, therefore, is to provide continuous replication of all persisted data. This can be done via storage replication or system replication. Storage replication uses integrated storage and is, therefore, only available in the SAP HANA TDI installation option. System replication is based on SAP HANA functionality in which changes are constantly replicated from the primary to the secondary system. In Chapter 5 we discuss storage and system replication, their advantages and disadvantages and what to consider when.

SAP HANA appliances are built for high availability. This is achieved by redundancy: redundancy in the hardware, software, network and data center design. In most cases, this is not enough. In Chapter 6 we look at high-availability software and how it can be used for single node and distributed SAP HANA systems.

Chapter 7 is on virtualization and SAP HANA. Both software and hardware virtualization is discussed. For software virtualization, we dive deeper into virtualization with VMware and IBM POWER as they are the hypervisors most commonly used with SAP HANA.

Throughout this book we explain the technology options available to deploy SAP HANA, the principles for backup and recovery, data replication, high-availability and virtualization, the things to consider and the available technology to choose from to implement a well-considered scenario.

We end with Chapter 8—Conclusion and Summary. In this chapter, we compare the different options and provide you with decision flowcharts which you can use in your organization to choose the proper technology for your environment and specific needs.

Acknowledgments

The first person I want to thank is Els Pollet who is the creator of every graph and schema to be found in this book. How many times did she have to start over because I forgot something or wanted something amended? My gratitude also goes to my colleagues at Logos Consulting. We are a small team, but we have more than a century of combined SAP technical experience between us. Our reference list of upgrades and migrations is breathtaking.

Finally, and most importantly, I want and need to thank my family and especially my wife, Ilka, who supported me in the writing of yet again another book.

My most sincere thanks also go to Alice Adams of Espresso Tutorials for her advice and support and to Karen Schoch who edited the manuscript until it was perfect.

We have added a few icons to highlight important information. These include:

Tips	
	Tips highlight information concerning more details about the subject being described and/or additional background information.

Attention	
	Attention notices draw attention to information that you should be aware of when you go through the examples from this book on your own.

Finally, a note concerning the copyright: all screenshots printed in this book are the copyright of SAP SE. All rights are reserved by SAP SE.

Copyright pertains to all SAP images in this publication. For simplification, we will not mention this specifically underneath every screenshot.

1 Architecture

SAP HANA is an in-memory database designed for high performance. In this chapter, we discuss the technology, use cases, the
on-premise delivery options and scalability.

Choosing a new hardware infrastructure for your critical business applications is never an easy task. Room for further growth, performance, and
high-availability are just a few aspects that need to be taken into consideration. It is even more complicated with SAP HANA as it has many requirements and prerequisites set by SAP for the hardware infrastructure.

1.1 Technology

SAP HANA is a database designed for high performance. All data is
compressed and kept in memory, which allows read operations to be
performed on massive data volumes without accessing disk, avoiding I/O
bottlenecks altogether.

What if I increase the memory of my traditional database server, will I get
the same performance increase?

No, you would probably not. The in memory is combined with SAP
HANA's column-based architecture. A column-based database needs
fewer operations than a traditional row-based database to get to the data
it needs. SAP HANA only needs to scan a single column, whereas a
traditional database needs to scan the complete row to get the data it
needs. This results in huge performance advantages compared to traditional databases.

1.2 Editions

SAP HANA is available on premise or in the cloud. All items discussed in
this book are applicable to the on-premise edition. In this section, we
briefly discuss the SAP HANA Cloud Platform and the SAP Cloud Integration editions.

1.2.1 SAP Cloud Platform

Basically, cloud means accessing applications and data over the Internet instead of on premise. The advantage lies in on-demand access to a pool of shared computing resources such as CPU, memory and network, which can rapidly be provisioned and made available with minimal effort. As with many applications, SAP HANA is available via the cloud, whether public or private.

SAP HANA Cloud Platform consists of the following options:

▶ SAP HANA Cloud or Enterprise Cloud
▶ SAP HANA One

SAP HANA Cloud or Enterprise Cloud

The SAP HANA Cloud offers infrastructure services to deploy SAP HANA systems quickly. This can be extended to databases or even applications as a service. Licensing is based on a monthly subscription. SAP HANA Enterprise Cloud (HEC) is an extension to the SAP HANA Cloud Platform. It is a privately managed cloud. Applications are delivered in the cloud as a managed service by SAP. Customers can either bring their existing SAP HANA and SAP applications licenses to be managed by SAP via these services or choose subscription-based access.

SAP HANA One

SAP HANA One is an SAP HANA system hosted in the public cloud and licensed on an hourly subscription. It is a perfect solution for small projects and startups as it provides them with an SAP HANA system at low cost.

1.2.2 SAP Cloud Integration

SAP HANA Cloud Integration is a cloud-based solution which enables customers to quickly and seamlessly connect cloud applications to SAP and non-SAP applications without programming. The solution delivers services to integrate business processes and data transfer between different companies and organizations. SAP HCI can be used to transfer data on-premise to cloud or cloud to cloud.

SAP HANA Cloud Integration provides the following features:

▶ runtime environment to extract, transform and load data between on-premise and the cloud

▶ connectivity support for IDOC, SOAP/HTTPS, SFTP and others

▶ security features such as encryption and certificate-based communication

▶ predefined integration content that covers most of the possible integration scenarios

The advantage of SAP HCI is that one platform, hosted centrally at SAP, can be used by independent customers in order to get their systems to exchange data with each other. The platform ensures that data related to different customers connected to SAP HCI is isolated. This is important, for example, when using SAP HCI for business-to-business scenarios.

SAP solutions such as Customer OnDemand and SuccessFactors make use of SAP HANA Cloud Integration.

1.2.3 SAP HANA Platform

The SAP HANA platform is composed of several components which are delivered in the different SAP HANA editions or bundles. There is the platform, or basis edition, and the options, which provide additional functions.

The SAP HANA platform edition is the technical foundation. It consists of the following components:

▶ SAP HANA Platform

▶ SAP HANA Database

▶ SAP HANA Client

▶ SAP HANA Studio

▶ SAP HANA XS Advanced Runtime

▶ SAP HANA XS Engine

▶ SAP HANA Advanced Data Processing

▶ SAP HANA Spatial

The SAP HANA options provide additional functions. An extra license is needed to use them:

- ▶ SAP HANA Accelerator for SAP ASE
- ▶ SAP HANA Advanced Data Processing
- ▶ SAP HANA Data Warehousing Foundation
- ▶ SAP HANA Dynamic Tiering
- ▶ SAP HANA Remote Data Sync
- ▶ SAP HANA Real-Time Replication
- ▶ SAP HANA Smart Data Streaming
- ▶ and many others

1.3 Use Cases

As already explained, SAP HANA is an in-memory column store-based database. But how does SAP-HANA fit into the existing SAP product offering? What are the SAP-HANA use cases?

Basically, the following SAP HANA use cases exist:

- ▶ as Primary Persistence for SAP NetWeaver-Based applications
- ▶ as Data Mart
- ▶ for access to live data
- ▶ as accelerator
- ▶ for smart data streaming
- ▶ as application and development platform

1.3.1 Primary Persistence for SAP NetWeaver-Based Applications

SAP NetWeaver is the core of any SAP system. All SAP Business Suite applications such as SAP ERP, SAP CRM and SAP BW and many others are built on the SAP Net Weaver platform.

SAP NetWeaver comes in two flavors—ABAP and JAVA. ABAP is the programming language in which most SAP Business Suite applications have been developed. JAVA is a programming language first released by

SUN microsystems in 1995. Most Internet applications and websites are built on JAVA.

The SAP NetWeaver ABAP and JAVA application servers are available on many databases such as Oracle, SQL-Server, Sybase, DB2 and, last but not least, SAP HANA. The SAP NetWeaver application server has been developed in such a way that it is database independent. SAP HANA is an exception. All SAP NetWeaver-based applications have been adapted not only to run on SAP HANA but also to capitalize on its advantages. This is accomplished by so-called push down optimizations. In the past, all data processing was done in the SAP application layer. The database was basically used as a container of data. Data manipulation was limited to select, insert and update. This is no longer the case with SAP HANA; the database layer also does data processing (see Figure 1.1).

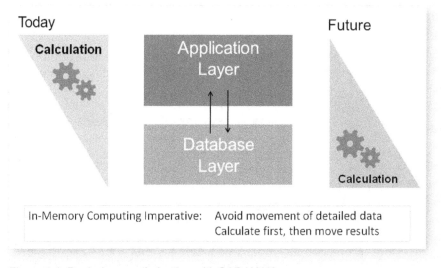

Figure 1.1: Push-down optimization with SAP HANA

There is one restriction, however. Dual-stack systems are not supported on SAP HANA. A dual-stack system is an SAP NetWeaver system in which ABAP and JAVA run together in the same instance. This restriction is, however, not that important. The installation of dual-stack systems is no longer supported as of NetWeaver Version 7.0. As of NetWeaver Version 7.4, dual-stack systems are no longer supported at all[1]. As such, any

---

[1] SAP Process Infrastructure is an exception. There is still a dual-stack 7.4 version.

dual-stack systems need to be split into an independent ABAP and JAVA system in any upgrade or migration project to SAP HANA.

1.3.2   Data Mart

A data mart is a repository of data gathered from different systems. This data forms the source of information for reporting.

What is the difference between a data mart and a business warehouse?

A data mart is a collection of data, comparable to a business warehouse. The difference is that a data mart focuses on answering a specific business problem. Because of this, a data mart is often able to more quickly adapt to changing business needs. The disadvantage is that several data marts might be needed to solve different business problems. This can lead to confusion because different data marts might offer a different point of view on comparable data.

Both data marts and business warehouses can use data from multiple sources and contain data which spans a large time period.

SAP HANA makes real-time analytics and reporting possible on data replicated from relational database systems using data marts. The data is copied from the traditional database into SAP HANA using replication technology. These replicated tables become the basis for specialized views that are created for analytical purposes.

1.3.3   Access to Live Data

SAP HANA Live is the successor of the SAP HANA Analytic Foundation and is a solution for real-time reporting on SAP HANA. SAP HANA Live comes with predefined content comparable to SAP BW content as calculation views for real-time reporting. Content exists for most ERP modules such as FI, CO, MM and many more.

The SAP HANA views can be accessed via applications such as SAP Business Objects. The added value in SAP HANA Live is that no development is needed. In ERP, if you need to create or modify a report, you need coding in ABAP. With SAP HANA live all you have to do is edit existing views provided by SAP or create new views.

SAP HANA Live can be installed in a side-by-side or integrated scenario.

Side-by-side scenario

In the side-by-side scenario, the database tables that are used by SAP HANA Live need to be replicated from the back-end system into the SAP HANA database. This is done using SAP Landscape Transformation Replication Server (see Chapter 2.3.1). Tables should only be created and data should only be replicated for those tables that are used in the analytical scenarios. This ensures that no unnecessary data is replicated and that no unnecessary DB memory is consumed.

Integrated scenario

In the integrated scenario, SAP ERP runs on the SAP HANA database. You do not need to create and replicate the database tables as they are already available in the SAP HANA database. They are maintained through the data dictionary of the corresponding ABAP Application Server. Therefore, all steps regarding table creation and data replication are not relevant in this scenario.

1.3.4   Accelerator

The SAP HANA accelerators extend the capabilities of SAP ERP by delivering performance, reporting and scalability features which are not possible with relational database systems.

The data is replicated between the standard database and SAP HANA. Depending on the scenario, the application knows whether to look for the data in the traditional database or in SAP HANA, using a secondary database connection.

SAP Supply Chain Management (SCM) or SAP Advanced Planning Optimizer (APO) have been using this principle for a very long time. Supply chain data is divided between two databases—a traditional database and SAP liveCache. SAP liveCache is an in-memory database with object-oriented database technology which can process enormous amounts of complex planning data. SAP liveCache can be considered the predecessor of SAP HANA.

The SAP HANA accelerator uses the same principle (see Figure 1.2). Data is replicated from the SAP ERP database to SAP HANA using replication technology. A secondary database connection needs to be set up in the SAP ERP system. The SAP HANA accelerators use this secondary connection to access data in the SAP HANA database.

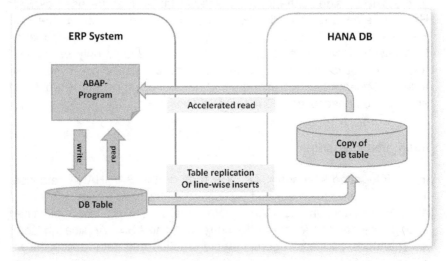

Figure 1.2: SAP HANA accelerator for FI/CO

Although many customers are already planning or are already in the process of migrating their SAP Business Suite applications to SAP HANA, customers can use the accelerators to achieve a fast return on investment. The SAP ERP "accelerated" transactions are available as part of the standard SAP system. The accelerators are an alternative for customers not ready to migrate to SAP HANA. SAP HANA is Unicode only. A migration to Unicode is not that complicated. It requires adapting the in house ABAP developments and interfaces to Unicode. Customers still running non-Unicode SAP systems can use the accelerators to start using SAP HANA functionality without migrating to Unicode. Technically, depending on the transaction executed, the SAP system opens a secondary database connection to the SAP HANA database.

1.3.5 Application Development Platform

SAP HANA can also be used as the basis for application development. In addition to the database, SAP HANA includes an application, a web server and a repository for content management, which all provide lifecycle functionality for development. SAP HANA Extended Application Services (XS) consists of development tools that allow applications to be built, which have an HTML or mobile application user interface.

Applications can also be built with .NET using Open Database Connectivity (ODBC) or JAVA using Java Database Connectivity (JDBC). These interface types provide methods for creating and maintaining connections, transactions, and other mechanisms for create, read, update, and delete operations in SAP HANA. These methods map directly to the underlying SQL semantics, hiding the actual communication details. Essentially, any application that can utilize ODBC, ODBO, or JDBC can integrate with SAP HANA.

1.4   On-Premise

SAP, traditionally an application vendor, entered the database market back in 2011 with the first release of SAP HANA. Although SAP already had MaxDB in their portfolio, they never made any serious attempts to position MaxDB as an alternative to the traditional database vendors such Microsoft and Oracle. Also, SAP bought Sybase back in 2010, but according to many analysts, SAP bought Sybase for its mobile technology, not for their database.

Instead of looking at the already existing database technology, SAP built the SAP HANA database from scratch, re-designing database technology altogether. SAP HANA was specifically built with high performance and data throughput in mind. All data is compressed and kept in memory, which allows read operations to be performed on massive data volumes without accessing disk. As a result, I/O latency is eliminated completely.

SAP HANA is also a column-based database whereas the traditional databases are row-based. This offers a huge performance improvement compared to traditional databases. By providing very fast performance for both read and write operations, the SAP HANA database supports transactional as well as analytical use cases. Finally, SAP HANA systems can be distributed across multiple servers to achieve good scalability in terms of both data volume and concurrent users.

On-premise SAP HANA is deployed in the following options:

▶ As an appliance—SAP HANA is delivered pre-installed and pre-configured on certified hardware. The SAP HANA hardware directory[2] lists all hardware solutions that have been certified by SAP.

---

[2] The SAP HANA hardware directory is available at *https://global.sap.com/ community/ebook/2014-09-02-hana-hardware/enEN/index.html*

► SAP HANA Tailored Datacenter Integration (TDI)—Compared with the appliance delivery approach, tailored data center integration is more open. It makes the integration of SAP HANA in an already existing data center more flexible. Basically, the appliance comes without storage, allowing it to be connected to the existing Storage Area Network (SAN).

The requirements for this deployment option are as follows:
► The server and storage solution are certified by SAP.
► The person performing the SAP HANA installation has passed SAP HANA installation certification.

1.4.1 Appliance

According to www.thefreedictionary.com, an appliance is "a device or instrument designed to perform a specific function". As an appliance, SAP HANA combines software components from SAP optimized on proven hardware provided by SAP's hardware partners. The appliance arrives with SAP HANA pre-installed, ready to go. Be aware that the operating system is always SUSE Linux Enterprise or Red Hat Enterprise Linux.

1.4.2 Tailored Datacenter Integration

The deployment of an appliance is easy but has its limitations. An appliance is an appliance. It consists of memory, CPU and storage. No more, no less. It is a standalone system and as such does not integrate with a storage or network solution which might already be in place.

The most important argument against appliances is that there is no integrated storage and, thus, no storage replication. The lack of integrated storage might have an impact on existing disaster recovery procedures, implying that customers need to rethink their business continuity procedures. In addition, virtualization without integrated storage is useless as the purpose of virtualization is the possibility to move a virtual system from one physical server to the next.

As an alternative to the appliance model, Tailored Datacenter Integration (TDI) targets the use of hardware and other infrastructure components already existing in a customer's landscape.

The Tailored Datacenter Integration option has the following advantages:

▶ It reduces hardware and operational costs by reusing existing hardware components and operation processes.

▶ It enables customers to reuse existing IT processes for SAP HANA.

Besides recognizing the benefits of SAP HANA TDI, keep in mind that the approach requires several tasks and prerequisites.

Enterprise Storage

What are the prerequisites of using SAP HANA Tailored Datacenter Integration with enterprise storage?

The SAP HANA server is exactly the same as the SAP HANA appliance but without storage. Note that only servers that are on the list of certified servers available for SAP HANA appliances are supported.

Keep the following best practices for SAP HANA servers in mind:

▶ No local disks or flash cards are required.

▶ Additional Fiber Channel adapters for a boot from a storage area network are recommended.

▶ The SAP HANA appliance certification applies. Servers which are only certified for single-node usage cannot be used for scale-out. Servers which have only been certified for a certain OS only, for example, SUSE Linux Enterprise (SLES), cannot be deployed on Red Hat Enterprise Linux (RHEL) and vice versa.

In addition:

▶ The storage solution must be certified for SAP HANA and must fulfill SAP's KPI's for data throughput and latency. SAP provides a tool named "SAP HANA Hardware Configuration Check Tool (HWCCT)". Customers can use it to measure data throughput and latency times between their SAP HANA computing nodes and their Enterprise Storage system. The official tool documentation is available as a PDF document attached to SAP Note 1943937.

▶ The SAP HANA installation needs to be done by a person who has successfully passed the exam "SAP Certified Technology Specialist (Edition 2015)—SAP HANA Installation" (E_HANAINS151). SAP HANA hardware partners and their employees do not need this certificate. However, companies, or their employees, who are sub-contractors of SAP HANA hardware partners must be certified to perform HANA SW installations.

Enterprise Network

As an in-memory database, SAP HANA uses multiple network connections to transfer data from applications to the database during standard operations: between the nodes in a scale-out solution, and between data centers in SAP HANA system replication. SAP HANA Tailored Datacenter Integration with enterprise network allows the setup of homogenous networks landscapes using the network components of a single vendor only.

The following best practices should be considered:

▶ The network solution must be certified for SAP HANA and must fulfill SAP's KPIs for data throughput and latency. SAP provides a tool named "SAP HANA Hardware Configuration Check Tool (HWCCT)". The official tool documentation is available as a PDF document attached to SAP Note 1943937.

▶ In addition, more recommendations about the setup of the networks inside and around an SAP HANA system can be found in the Network Requirements whitepaper[3].

Table 1.1 compares the SAP HANA appliance with the Tailored Datacenter Integration option. Both options have advantages and disadvantages. The most important advantages of an appliance are: it is an integrated solution, comes pre-installed and configured, and is fully supported by SAP. The largest disadvantage is the lack of integrated storage, which is not the case with SAP HANA TDI. TDI, on the other hand, tends to be more complex as many components need to be glued together and it lacks the single point of contact for support that the appliance has.

For the overall integration between the different components, support is divided among: SAP, the storage and network vendor, and the customer—you.

The key advantage of the SAP TDI option is standardization. Appliances are unmanageable in large SAP landscapes. As technology advances,

---

[3] The SAP HANA TDI Network Requirements document is available at
http://scn.sap.com/docs/DOC-63221

each new appliance comes with new components resulting in system management procedures which need to be adapted.

	Appliance	TDI
Hardware	► Choose your HW partner ► Existing hardware cannot be used	► Use preferred or existing storage ► Use preferred or existing network
Implementation	► Pre-configured and pre-installed ► Implementation cost is low	► Only HW is delivered ► Installation done by customer or external consultants
Certification	► Guaranteed by SAP and HW partner	► SAP HANA Going-Live Check by SAP ► SAP HANA HW Configuration Check Tool
Support	► Provided by SAP	► Provided by the individual HW providers

Table 1.1: SAP HANA Appliance versus SAP TDI

True, not all applications are alike. SAP ERP has different requirements to SAP SCM and their roles (such as production, test or development) reflect different business scenarios that influence the technical requirements, and, as a result, the design of the architecture. However, in an SAP context, these applications run on the SAP NetWeaver platform, which technically behaves the same no matter which application is running on it, and makes standardization feasible.

Standardization is important and brings the following advantages:

► reduces software and hardware costs
► lowers risk
► increases productivity
► minimizes staff training time and expense
► manages change effectively

Standardization is possible vertically by limiting the duplication of business functions and reducing modifications or deployments of too many applications. It is also possible horizontally by choosing the technology standard thus reducing the choice of servers, network, and storage components across multiple applications. By standardizing your architecture both vertically and horizontally, you will significantly reduce the complexity of your system landscape.

In addition to standardization, SAP TDI also has advantages when it comes to automation, disaster recovery and exception handling:

- ▶ Automation—SAP TDI in combination with virtualization eliminates unnecessary and repetitive manual intervention or IT tasks, such as deployment of new SAP HANA instances, through automation, which takes advantage of standardization to reduce risk and improve productivity with consistent results.
- ▶ Disaster Recovery—It eliminates the single point of failure by using storage replication and virtualization.
- ▶ Exception handling—In large SAP landscapes, exceptions are unavoidable. Different SLA demands for different applications can sometimes make it hard to fit everything into one standardized model. This requires a process for evaluating requests for exceptional solutions, documenting the exceptions, and doing this continuously.

1.5 Capacity Planning

The choice of hardware resources is a balance between adequate performance and acceptable cost. Proper hardware sizing is complicated, but important, and should not be neglected. There are many things to consider and in greenfield projects, assumptions need to be made.

1.5.1 Quick Sizer

SAP developed the Quick Sizer to assist customers and consultants with proper hardware sizing. With the Quick Sizer you can translate business requirements into technical requirements. It consists of a questionnaire which is based on business-oriented figures such as how many invoices or sales documents you will process per hour. When done, the Quick Sizer calculates CPU; disk; memory and I/O resource categories based on a throughput number; and the number of users working concurrently with the SAP system in a number of SAPs. The number of SAPs is a hardware and database independent figure. Compare it to horsepower in the automobile world. Hardware vendors have the tools and procedures to translate the number of SAPs into the hardware resources needed.

1.5.2 Sizing Reports

For existing customers, there is the SAP HANA sizing reports. There is a sizing report for SAP ERP, SAP CRM, SAP SRM and SAP SCM and there is a different sizing report for SAP BW.

Sizing for the SAP ABAP Application Server?

 The SAP sizing reports only take SAP HANA into account. SAP doesn't expect any changes concerning CPU, memory and network requirements for the SAP ABAP Application Server. This means that the existing hardware and network infrastructure can still be used. This is the default when doing an SAP upgrade combined with a migration to SAP HANA (DMO project). The SAP system is upgraded to the latest version while the data is migrated from any database to SAP HANA. The SAP ABAP Application Server remains where it is, on the existing hardware infrastructure.

Sizing Report for SAP Business Suite Systems

For SAP Business Suite Systems such as SAP ERP, SAP CRM, SAP SRM and SAP SCM, the ABAP report estimates the memory and disk space requirements for database tables. The report is available through SAP Note 1872170 - Suite on HANA - S/4 sizing report. The report can be installed in any system as of SAP_BASIS 6.20. It is also included in the support tools; ST-PI_2008_620-710 SP09 and ST-PI 740 SP00 and above.

The report estimates the maximum memory consumption of the database if migrated to SAP HANA.

In addition, the report:

▶ is independent of the source database provider,

▶ considers distribution of tables to row/column store,

- ▶ considers de-clustering / de-pooling,
- ▶ considers differences for secondary indexes,
- ▶ considers compression of legacy database, Unicode conversion,
- ▶ can be used for sizing of all products running on SAP NetWeaver ABAP.

The report behaves differently depending on the system to be sized. Options such as "Perform sizing of S/4 HANA or S/4 HANA finance" will not be visible if your system is not suitable for S/4 HANA (for example, when using the report on a CRM system).

Go to transaction SA38 or SE38 and execute report /SDF/HDB_SIZING (see Figure 1.3).

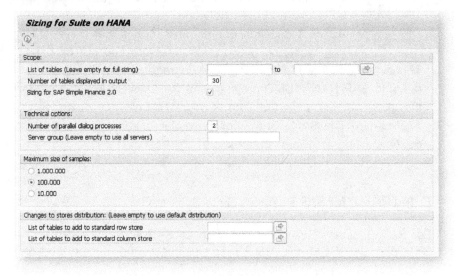

Figure 1.3: Sizing for Suite on HANA, sizing report

Most options can be left as default when sizing a standard SAP system:

- ▶ Leave the "list of tables" empty when sizing the entire database.
- ▶ The number of parallel processes can be increased when sizing a large system. Note that free dialog processes will be needed for each task.
- ▶ The size of the samples can be left default. A maximum of 100.000 records per table is representative enough.

As the report scans the whole database, it might take a long time to complete. It should therefore be started in the background.

Figure 1.4 is the output of the sizing report as run on an SAP ERP system, in this example, an appliance with 3TB of memory would be sufficient.

```
RESULTS OF SUITE ON HANA SIZING IN GB

Based on the selected table(s), the anticipated maximum memory requirement is

for Suite on HANA:
- Total memory requirement                                    2.244,1
- Net data size on disk                                       1.545,4

for Suite on HANA with Simple Finance 2.0:
- Total memory requirement                                    2.275,2
- Net data size on disk                                       1.628,5

for SoH considering reduction potential:
- Total memory requirement                                    1.812,8
- Net data size on disk                                       1.585,6
```

Figure 1.4: Results of Suite on HANA Sizing

For more information on the sizing report for SAP ERP on HANA and for S4/HANA see the Questions and Answers document attached to SAP Note 1872170. Always install the latest version of the report as more and more features are added as time passes.

Sizing Report for SAP Business Warehouse systems

Report /SDF/HANA_BW_SIZING can be used to estimate the memory requirements after the migration to SAP HANA for an SAP BW system. The latest version of the BW Sizing report comes with SAP Note 2296290 – New Sizing Report for BW on HANA. The report requires ST-PI 2008_1_7xx SP8 or ST-PI 740 and SAP NetWeaver BW 7.0 SP 1 or higher.

The report has the following characteristics:

▶ calculates table sizes based on sampled data in ABAP memory and total record count

▶ calculates the additional space needed if the source system is still non-Unicode

▶ takes source database compression into account taken

- ▶ takes separation of tables in row store and column store into account
- ▶ calculates overall SAP HANA memory requirements with table type specific compression factors
- ▶ takes future resource requirements into account based on a relative or absolute yearly growth
- ▶ can take a subset of the system or entire system into account
- ▶ can take SAP HANA Dynamic Tiering into account
- ▶ can be executed in parallel to speed up processing parallel processing of tables to speed up processing time.

The options and selections of the sizing report are breathtaking (see Figure 1.5).

Determine DB size relevant for BW on HANA Sizing

General

Store output in file	X	File name	HANA_Sizing.txt
Number of parallel procs	4		
Suppress tables < 1MB	X		
Unload inactive tables	X		
Target Release 7.40	✓		

Precision

High	○
Medium	○
Low	⦿

Scenario / Subset Selection

Use system subset only	☐		
List of top level InfoProv.		to	
Subset for existing BW system	○		
New BW system using this subset	⦿		
Exclude listed objects	○		

Future Growth Simulation

Consider Growth	☐
Number of years	3
Relative growth (in %)	⦿
Absolute growth (in GB)	○
Growth value	

Non-active Data

Consider non-active data	✓	
WARM write-optimized DSOs		to

Dynamic Tiering

Use Dynamic Tiering	☐	
Objects in Dynamic Tiering		to

Figure 1.5: Sizing report for BW on HANA

Fortunately, the SAP BW on SAP HANA sizing document, which is attached to SAP Note 2296290 explains them in detail.

The most important options are:

- ▶ Number of parallel processes; sizing a large BW system takes time. It is therefore strongly recommended to run the report in parallel. You only need to make sure that a sufficient number dialog processes are available. If not enough dialog processes are available; the degree of parallelism will be automatically reduced.

- ▶ Precision settings; higher precision settings result in more detailed sampling and high runtimes. Precision "Low" is sufficient in most cases. Setting "High" is recommended for systems smaller then 500GB.

- ▶ Scenario and subset selection; this flag can be set to only consider a subset of the BW system. Objects such as InfoCubes, InfoObjects, DataStores can be specified. The option 'Subset for existing BW system' can be set if you want to move some of the data to an already existing BW system on SAP HANA and only need to calculate the extra amount of memory needed. Option 'New BW system using this subset' will calculate the same, but will also include the system tables required to run a BW system on SAP HANA. Use this option to migrate the subset to a new BW system.

- ▶ Options for further growth; should further growth be included in the report? If so, should it be relative, a percentage to the current size or an absolute growth in GB and over how many years?

- ▶ Dynamic Tiering; with this option, Dynamic Tiering can be considered in the calculation. A list of objects needs to be supplied which are supposed to be stored in the Dynamic Tiering SAP HANA instance.

The sizing report for BW can be configured so that it only considers memory configurations that your hardware partners offers (see Figure 1.6). From this list; you will get a minimum configuration and a recommended configuration, depending on the sizing results.

For the selected memory configurations, the report considers:

- ▶ A minimum configuration which can store all data in a single node taking future growth into account.

- ► A recommended configuration, which takes scale-up and scale-out into account. Scale-out scenarios with more then 8 nodes will be avoided.
- ► Recommendations with an expected utilization of the memory on any node close to its capacity are avoided.
- ► Later versions of the report allow custom memory sizes to be supplied. This to support variable LPAR configurations on IBM Power platforms.

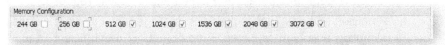

Figure 1.6: Sizing report for BW on HANA, appliances to consider

Listing 1.1 is the output of the sizing report as run on an SAP BW system. In this case, a scale-out environment with 5 nodes of 512GB would be the minimum, 3 nodes of 1024GB would be recommended.

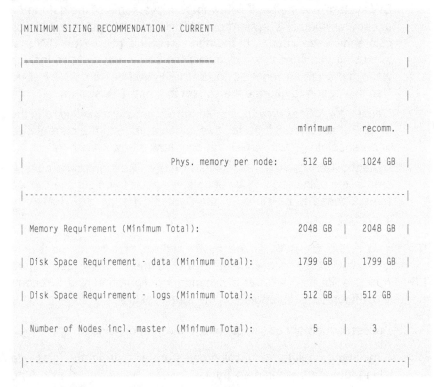

Listing 1.1: Minimum sizing recommendations

Minimum vs. Recommended

 SAP HANA prefers a small set of nodes with less memory over a single node with more memory for cost effectiveness and flexibility reasons. Minimum memory amount is determined by requirements for the master node.

1.5.3 Easy and Lazy Sizing

You can use the following formula to get a rough estimate of the required memory for SAP HANA, if adequate sizing is of no concern or if your source system is too old for the sizing reports:

```
SAP HANA memory = (Net Data Size anyDB / 2) × 1,2
               (20% safety buffer) + 50GB
```

The formula consists of the following components:

▶ The database size of the source database; you can use the standard SAP database tools (transaction DBACOCKPIT) to get the size of the database. The formula assumes that the database is uncompressed. In SAP HANA, all data is compressed thanks to the column store, which allows for extensive compression. As such, you can assume that the SAP HANA memory footprint will be 50% of the current database size.

▶ Better be safe than sorry, SAP recommends to add a 20% safety margin.

▶ The code stack and services of SAP HANA uses 50GB.

For example, a 1TB database, would have a 1024GB/2 × 1,2 + 50GB or 660GB memory footprint. Keep in mind that not all memory is available to SAP HANA. The operating system needs roughly 10% of the first 64GB of memory and another 3% of the remaining memory. In our example the server would at least need 700GB of main memory. As such, an appliance of 768GB memory would be sufficient.

Mind the Delta Merges!

Extra memory is needed for the delta merges. The impact should not be underestimated if there are huge tables in your system. This is the case in SAP ERP systems in which the utilities or safety health and environment components are used. As a rule of thumb, add the size of the two largest tables to the "Net Data Size anyDB" parameter.

Consider future growth. Estimate your yearly growth rate. The SAP Database Cockpit contains historic data on database growth, which can be used as input. Another source of information could be the Early Watch Alert, which includes detailed database information such as database growth.

CPU

Verify the CPU consumption of your current database to get an idea about the future CPU requirements. You can use SAP's monitoring or operating system tools to do so. SAP HANA does a lot in parallel to guarantee optimal response times. This is especially beneficial in analytical applications. You should therefore multiple your current CPU consumption by 3. This formula is also applicable to OLTP applications. Additional CPU resources will be needed when SAP HANA Enterprise Search is to be used.

Storage

SAP HANA needs storage! To give a prediction of the required disk space, you have to take the current net size and the disk space for delta merges into account. During a delta merge, the table is temporarily duplicated on disk. The space needed is calculated by taking the sum of the two biggest tables and including them in the calculation. On top, you should add 25GB for the space required for the statistics server.

The final formula looks like:

```
HANA disk space (Total Net Disk Space) = (Net Data Size
  anyDB + Disk Space for Merges) / 4 (compression) × 1,2
              (20% safety buffer) + 25GB
```

If you are using SAP HANA Enterprise Search, you should add 20% disk resources on top.

It should be understood that the Easy & Lazing Sizing methodology is not recommended. It should only be used to get a rough idea about the memory footprint.

1.5.4   T-Shirt Sizing

SAP has defined T-shirt sizes for SAP HANA to both simplify sizing and to limit the number of hardware configurations supported, thus reducing complexity. Customers can use the result of the sizing report to select the SAP HANA T-shirt size that matches their requirements.

Table 1.2 lists the T-shirt sizes for SAP HANA.

SAP T-shirt Size	XS	S / S+	M/ M+	L
Memory	128GB	256GB	512GB	1TB
CPUs	2	2	4	8
SAS/SSD for data volumes	1TB	1TB	4TB	4TB
SAS/SDD for log volumes	128GB	256GB	512GB	1TB

Table 1.2: T-Shirt sizes for SAP HANA

For example, a sizing result of 400 GB for the main memory suggests a T-shirt size of M.

The T-shirt sizes S+ and M+ are upgradable versions of S and M sizes:

▶ S+ delivers capacity equivalent to S, but the hardware is upgradable to an M size.

▶ M+ delivers capacity equivalent to M, but the hardware is upgradable to an L size.

In addition to these standard T-shirt sizes, which apply to all cases of SAP HANA, there are configurations that are limited for use with SAP Business Suite applications powered by SAP HANA (see Table 1.3).

SAP T-shirt Size	L	XL	XXL
Memory	1TB	2TB	4TB
CPUs	4	8	8
SAS/SSD for data volumes	4TB	8TB	16TB
SAS/SDD for log volumes	1TB	2TB	4TB

Table 1.3: T-Shirt sizes for SAP Business Suite on SAP HANA

The workload for the SAP Business Suite applications has different characteristics. It is less CPU bound and more memory-intensive than standard SAP HANA workload. Therefore, the memory per core ratio is different to the standard T-shirt sizes.

1.5.5   Infrastructure Sizing

The result of the memory sizing, whether done via the QuickSizer or the sizing reports, is the basis for the hardware recommendation for an SAP HANA system. The approach for an SAP appliance differs from an SAP TDI approach. In the first case, it is up to the certified hardware vendor to map the sizing result to a certified appliance. In the latter, it is up to the customer to map the result against servers, network and storage.

Appliance

For those customers who want to go for the appliance approach, there is a selection of certified appliances and hardware partners to choose from[4]. You only need to verify that the appliance matches the memory sizing result. Storage and CPU sizing should not be considered, as they are included in the certified appliance offering.

In fact, the number of CPU's is based on the core-to-memory (CTM) formula, whereas the size of storage is based on a memory-to-disk calculation:

▶ The capacity for the data volumes is calculated based on the total amount of memory (RAM) multiplied by 4.

$$DISK = 4 \times RAM$$

▶ The minimum size of the log volume is equal to the amount of memory (RAM).

$$DISK\ LOG = 1 \times RAM$$

Tailored Datacenter Integration

With SAP Tailored Datacenter Integration (SAP TDI) customers can re-use an already existing storage or network solution in combination with an SAP HANA appliance. In the TDI scenario, SAP HANA appliances come without storage and can be connected to the already existing storage or network solution.

The SAP TDI approach has the following requirements:

▶ Only uses certified servers. The same memory sizing reports can be used to estimate the memory footprint.
▶ The storage and network solution needs to be certified by SAP.

---

[4] The SAP HANA hardware directory is available at *https://global.sap.com/ community/ebook/2014-09-02-hana-hardware/enEN/index.html*

▶ As there are no disks in the appliances, they cannot come pre-installed. The installation needs to be done on-site by an SAP HANA engineer certified for installations.

SAP HANA is an in-memory database which stores and processes the bulk of its data in memory. Additionally, it provides protection against data loss by saving the data in persistent storage locations.

So, how much storage do we need for SAP HANA? The sizing reports only cover the memory requirement. How does the memory requirement translate to storage requirements?

SAP HANA uses storage for several purposes:

▶ SAP HANA persists a copy of the in-memory data by writing changed data in the form of so-called save-point to disk.

▶ As with any database system, to ensure that the database can be recovered, SAP HANA records every transaction in the redo log.

▶ SAP HANA installation, binaries, libraries and support scripts: SAP HANA stores configuration files and by default traces files to this location.

▶ SAP HANA needs backups. These might be written to storage or to a third-party backup location.

▶ A storage location for database exports. This is only needed for troubleshooting and diagnostic purposes.

Only SAP HANA in TDI is considered here

 The sizing recommendations in this section are only valid for the SAP HANA Tailored Datacenter Integration (TDI) approach. Sizing requirements for SAP HANA appliances are not discussed here as they come pre-installed with memory, CPU and storage as sized by the hardware vendor.

The sizing reports, which exist for SAP Suite, S4/HANA and SAP BW on SAP HANA, give a good indication of the required memory. For greenfield implementations, the SAP QuickSizer can be used.

The latest versions of the sizing reports return two values to be taken into account for memory sizing and disk sizing (see Figure 1.7):

MEMORY SIZING CALCULATION DETAILS	HANA SIZE IN GB
Column store data	174,9
+ Row store data	36,9
= Anticipated memory requirement for the initial data	211,7
+ Cached Hybrid LOB (20%)	20,2
+ Work space	211,7
+ Fixed size for code, stack and other services	50,0
= Anticipated initial memory requirement for HANA	493,7

DISK SIZING CALCULATION DETAILS	HANA SIZE IN GB
Column store data	174,9
+ Row store data	36,9
+ hybrid LOBs	101,1
+ Space required for merges	48,0
+ Metadata and statistics	25,0
= Initial net data size on disk	385,8

Figure 1.7: Memory sizing calculation, details

the total memory requirement, which includes:

▶ row store data

▶ column store data

▶ temporary data for objects created dynamically at runtime (e.g. when merging deltas or when executing queries)

▶ code, stack and other services

▶ hybrid LOB records which are cached in memory

the anticipated net data size on disk, which consists of two parts:

▶ the net data size on disk

▶ the disk space required during "Delta Merge" processes

Disk Space Required for the Data Volume

SAP HANA saves in-memory data to disk under /hana/data/<SID>. The recommended size of the data volume for a given SAP HANA system is equal to the anticipated net disk space plus an additional free space of 20%:

```
Size data = 1.2 × net disk space for data
```

More space is needed during the migration to SAP HANA

During the migration of a non-HANA database to SAP HANA, the system may temporarily need more disk space for data than calculated in the sizing phase.

Disk Space Required for the Log Volume

The default location of the log segments is /hana/log/<SID>. The size of the volume depends on the number of data changes between save points. Save points are created every 5 minutes. The more changes executed during two save points, the more redo log segments are written to the log volume.

The following behavior should be taken into account when it comes to the log volume:

- ▶ Save points may be delayed during high workloads. The amount of redo logs in the log volume will grow until a save point is completed or until the log segments are full.
- ▶ If the log mode is set to normal, which should be the case for production systems, the redo log is not overwritten until a backup has taken place.

There is no correlation between the SAP HANA database size and the required log volume size. The size of the log volume depends on the amount of changes. The following formula is based on best practices by SAP and is based on the total memory requirement of the SAP system:

```
[systems < 512GB ] "Size redolog" = 1/2 × RAM
[systems > 512GB ] "Size redolog(min)" = 512GB
```

Using the formula above, a 256GB system would need a 128GB log volume. For a 1TB and 2TB system, a 512GB log volume would be sufficient.

Size with caution!

 For large databases, the formula above represents a minimum value. The amount of data stored in the log volume depends on the workload processed. There might be cases where this value is not sufficient.

Disk Space Required for SAP HANA Installation

All binary, trace and configuration files are stored on a file system, `/hana/shared/<SID>`. These are static. It is the trace files which require additional space. The sizes of the trace files depend on the total memory requirement.

For single-node SAP HANA systems, the recommended disk space is:

```
"Size installation (single-node)" = MIN(1 × RAM), MAX (1TB)
```

For example, a single-node 512GB system needs 512GB for its trace files, whereas a 2TB system could consume up to 1TB.

For scale-out SAP HANA systems, the recommended disk space depends on the number of worker nodes. For every four worker nodes of a given scale-out system, a disk space of 1x RAM of one worker is recommended.

```
Size installation(scale-out) = 1 × RAM_of_worker per
                    4 worker nodes
```

Some examples:

- ▶ 4-node scale-out system (3 workers + 1 standby) of 512GB per node = 1 × 512GB
- ▶ 6-node scale-out system (5 workers + 1 standby) of 512GB per node = 2 × 512GB or 1TB
- ▶ 10-node scale-out system (9 workers + 1 standby) of 1TB per node = 3 × 1TB = 3TB

Disk Space Required for Backups

The amount of space needed for the backup directory is based on the total size of the data volumes, the frequency with which data is changed in the SAP HANA database and the backup policy. The number and size of the log backups depend on the number of changes in the database.

```
Size backups = (Size data + Size redo log) × number of days
               which need to be kept on disk.
```

This formula does not take incremental or differential backups into account. The footprint of these depends on the number of changes since the last full or incremental backup.

NFS might be a performance bottleneck!

 Backups of several SAP HANA systems can be written to a network file system. This might have an impact on data throughput and the duration of the backups when doing them in parallel if the storage cannot guarantee a constant level of throughput.

Disk Space Required for Exports

A database export might be needed from time to time to analysis the root cause of a problem. Sufficient disk space should be foreseen for this as well. In most cases, it is not necessary to export the entire database content for root cause analysis. Therefore, as a rule of thumb, it should be sufficient to reserve storage space of about two times the size of the biggest database table.

Others

10 GB of disk space is a minimum for the Linux Operating System. 50GB is more appropriate. Additionally, at least 50 GB must be provided for the /usr/sap file system as this is the place where other SAP software that supports SAP HANA will be installed. It is possible to join this location with the Linux installation.

So, what do you do if your sizing is all wrong? If you have oversized, too bad, you'll lose money. At least your end-users won't complain. But, what if you have undersized? This is where scale-up and scale-out come in (see Chapter 3).

1.6 Data Tiering

SAP-HANA systems are expensive because such fast access to busi-ness data is expensive. The question one might ask is, "do we need fast access to all the data all the time"? The cost of keeping all data in memory may not be justifiable anymore. Slower response times when accessing rare or old data may be acceptable. There is another option, such as SAP data archiving. If you have it, fine, if not, it should be con-sidered a separate project which is mostly business related. SAP data archiving is not something which can be implemented quickly.

Fortunately, different solutions are possible with SAP HANA to manage the size of required hardware, limiting either the required memory or even the whole database size.

The following options are available, still allowing data access with decent performance:

- ▶ near-line storage (NLS)
- ▶ Dynamic Tiering
- ▶ integration with Hadoop

The SAP HANA Data Warehousing Foundation

 The SAP HANA Data Warehousing Foundation or DWF is a series of tools for large-scale SAP HANA installati-ons that support data management and distribution within an SAP HANA landscape.

SAP DWF can be used to optimize the memory footprint of an SAP HANA system by using solutions such as SAP IQ, SAP HANA Dyna-mic Tiering and Hadoop (Spark SQL). SAP DWF can be used toge-ther with SAP BW on SAP HANA, SAP HANA Agile Data Mart and many others. With Data Lifecycle Manager, SAP DWF provides an SAP HANA XS-based tool to relocate data in native SAP HANA to storage locations such as SAP IQ, SAP HANA Dynamic Tiering opti-on or Hadoop (Spark SQL). For this purpose, Data Lifecycle Manager enables SAP HANA administrators to model aging rules on persis-tence objects (SAP HANA tables).

1.6.1 Near-line Storage (NLS) for SAP BW

With Near-Line Storage (NLS), cold or rarely used data is moved out of the SAP HANA database to a separate SAP IQ system which is installed on a cheaper storage solution reducing the memory footprint of SAP-HANA (see Figure 1.8). SAP IQ is a disk-oriented database and needs far less memory than SAP HANA.

The adapter for SAP IQ is delivered with the SAP BW system. This allows access to hot and cold data to be fully transparent to the application and end-users. The only thing an end-user might experience is a slower response time when accessing cold data.

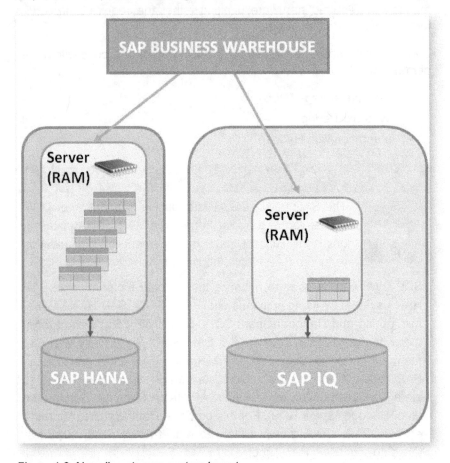

Figure 1.8: Near-line storage system layout

As SAP IQ is installed on separate hardware, technical operations for both systems can be decoupled. Disaster recovery can vary; one may use a replication solution for the SAP HANA system and just a back-up/restore-based solution for the SAP IQ system.

SAP IQ is available in a simplex and multiplex architecture.

Simplex

The SAP IQ Simplex layout consists of an SAP IQ server running on a single node. In this configuration, the files are located on the host machine on which the SAP IQ server is running.

Multiplex

SAP IQ Multiplex are multiple SAP IQ servers acting as one. Every node runs on a dedicated host. Every node has dedicated temporary storage and a catalog store. The IQ store is shared among all nodes. The primary node or coordinator manages all read-write transactions and maintains the global catalog.

Near-line Storage (NLS) and SAP IQ Multiplex

 The SAP IQ Multiplex architecture is not yet supported with SAP Near Line Storage (NLS)!

1.6.2 Dynamic Tiering

SAP HANA Dynamic tiering is a solution for big data. Dynamic tiering adds disk-based extended storage to your SAP HANA database. Data tiering is done via the SAP HANA Dynamic Tiering Service. This service can be used to create extended stores for extended tables. Extended tables behave like all other SAP HANA tables, but their data resides in the disk-based extended store or warm store. Dynamic data tiering can reduce the size of required memory.

The application determines which tier to save data to: the in-memory store (the hot store) or extended storage (the warm store). Warm or often-accessed data remains in memory whereas cooler or less-accessed data is saved in the extended store.

For production, SAP HANA and SAP HANA Dynamic Tiering require separate dedicated hosts. This is not the case for non-production systems for which you can install SAP HANA and SAP HANA Dynamic Tiering on the same host.

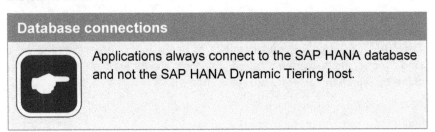

Database connections

Applications always connect to the SAP HANA database and not the SAP HANA Dynamic Tiering host.

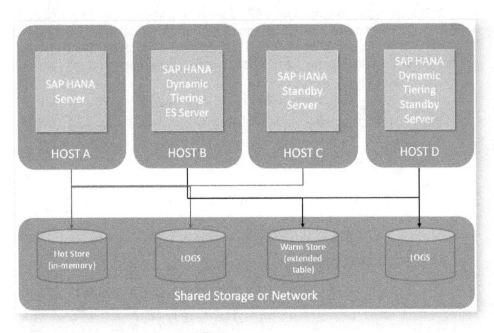

Figure 1.9: SAP HANA Dynamic Tiering

SAP HANA and the dynamic tiering host share a common database, comprised of regular and extended tables. The system layout consists of an SAP HANA instance and a dynamic tiering host or ES server. High availability can be achieved by installing a secondary or standby dynamic tiering host (see Figure 1.9).

The SAP HANA Database platform

SAP HANA Dynamic Tiering is a component of the SAP HANA database platform and part of SAP's Big Data offering.

1.6.3 Hadoop

Apache Hadoop, or Hadoop, is an open source java-based framework that supports the processing of large data sets in a distributed computing environment. Hadoop is a distributed file system designed to scale up from a single to a thousand servers. It is designed to run on computers which do not share anything, even though data will be distributed among all the available nodes. High availability is done in the design, as data is stored to more than one copy store. Instead of relying on high-end hardware and software clusters, failures are detected and handled in the application layer.

Hadoop has many advantages:

▶ scalability—new nodes can be added as required

▶ cost—commodity servers can be used which reduces the cost per terabyte enormously

▶ flexibility—any type of data, structured or unstructured, can be stored on Hadoop

▶ high availability—data is stored to more than one node. If a node is lost, data processing can continue

Hadoop is not a database!

Hadoop is an efficient, distributed file system and not a database. The Hadoop Distributed File System (HDFS) is the file system that spans all the nodes in a Hadoop cluster for data storage. It links together the file systems on many local nodes to make them into one big file system. HDFS assumes nodes will fail, so it achieves reliability by replicating data across multiple nodes.

SAP HANA can be integrated with Hadoop, which brings the following added values:

▶ storing structured and unstructured data such as system and web logs, text data, audio and video data on cheaper data storage

▶ access to data, for which performance is less critical, on cheaper data storage

▶ data can be kept over a longer period, although access time is slower

▶ fault tolerance and scalability is built into Hadoop by design

The SAP HANA Hadoop connector can be used to pull data from Hadoop to SAP HANA or vice versa. The SAP HANA Data Warehousing Foundation, Data Lifecycle Manager, supports bi-directional data relocation. Data can be relocated from SAP HANA to storage locations in Hadoop and the other way around. You can model aging rules on SAP HANA tables in order to relocate "aged" or less frequently used data from SAP HANA tables in native SAP HANA applications.

What about SAP HANA Vora?

 SAP HANA Vora is an engine which runs on the Hadoop cluster. It was designed to make data from Hadoop more accessible and usable. Hadoop offers low-cost storage for huge amounts of data. However, the data is unstructured which makes it difficult to handle. SAP HANA Vora builds hierarchies for the Hadoop data and enables OLAP style in-memory analysis.

2 Landscape Layout

Options, options, options. There are many options for the deployment of SAP HANA systems. There is the standard or standalone SAP HANA system (SCOS), multitenant database containers (MDC), multiple components on one database (MCOD), multiple components on one system (MCOS) and finally virtualization for SAP HANA.

There are various aspects influencing the choice between the different deployment options. The impact on high-availability and disaster recovery needs to be considered and the required software change management landscape with its development, testing, quality assurance and production systems has to be mapped to SAP HANA hardware infrastructure.

2.1 Deployment

This section discusses the various different types of technical deployment options (see Figure 2.1), such as:

- ▶ single application on one SAP HANA system (SCOS)
- ▶ multitenant database containers (MDC)
- ▶ multiple applications on one SAP HANA system (MCOD)
- ▶ multiple SAP HANA systems on one host (MCOS)
- ▶ SAP HANA with virtualization

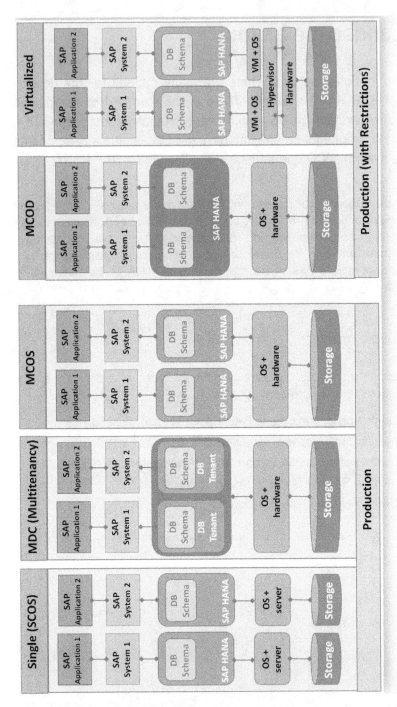

Figure 2.1: SAP HANA deployment options

2.1.1 Single Application on One SAP HANA System (SCOS)

The standard SAP HANA deployment is a single SAP HANA application running in a single database schema in a single SAP HANA database as part of an SAP HANA system or, as SAP calls it, a single application on one SAP HANA system (SCOS). This is a simple, straightforward scenario that is supported for all scenarios without restriction.

For example, two SAP HANA appliances are sufficient for a two-system SAP BW landscape (development and production). There is no failover for the production system in this setup. This might be acceptable for customers where reporting is not considered business critical.

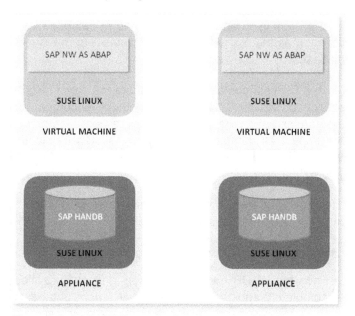

Figure 2.2: SAP HANA standard deployment option

The standard SAP HANA deployment option (see Figure 2.2) is a system layout which was often used in the early days of SAP HANA and is still used by customers who are only deploying SAP HANA for a limited use case such as SAP BW.

Note that in the example above, only the SAP HANA database is installed on the appliance. The SAP NetWeaver application server is deployed on a different, in this case, virtual machine running on SUSE Enterprise Linux.

49

2.1.2   Multitenant Database Containers (MDC)

SAP HANA supports multiple isolated databases in a single SAP HANA system. These are referred to as multitenant database containers. The multitenant database container setup of SAP HANA is comparable to the SQL-Server or Sybase instance layout. There is an SAP HANA instance, a system database and several tenant databases. The system database is used for central system administration. It is also the database from which recoveries of the tenant databases are initiated.

An SAP HANA system installed in multiple-container mode is identified by a single system ID (SID). An SID and a database name identify databases. From an administration perspective, there is a distinction between tasks performed at system level and those performed at database level. Database clients, such as the SAP HANA studio, connect to the system or the tenant databases.

All the databases in a multiple-container system share the same installation of database system software, the same computing resources, and the same system administration. As a result, software upgrades or system maintenance impact all databases. In addition, system replication applies to the whole SAP HANA instance; that is, for all tenant databases including the system database.

Newly created tenant databases are automatically integrated into the replication process after they are backed up.

However, each database is fully isolated when it comes to:

▶ Security—Each tenant DB has its own users and authorizations which are completely separate from the other tenant databases. The database catalog and repository are also isolated in each tenant DB.

▶ Backups—With SAP HANA multitenant database containers, if each application is deployed on its own tenant DB, then each can be backed up and recovered independently.

▶ Moving and copying tenant DB's—Tenant databases can be moved or copied using the backup and restore capabilities. This only needs downtime for the tenant database affected. The other tenant databases can stay online. Simply perform a backup and then either create a new tenant database and restore the backup into this tenant database, or restore the copy into an existing tenant database.

▶ Traces and logs—Each tenant database has his own set of trace and log files.

In general, all applications that are supported to run on a single database SAP HANA system are also supported to run on an MDC system. Tools exist to convert a single-container system to a multiple-container system.

Many customers use MDC to consolidate several SAP HANA databases into one SAP HANA system. This setup minimizes the number of appliances and reduces total cost of ownership (TCO).

Consider the following example:

The customer has SAP ERP, SAP PO and SAP CRM landscapes. Every landscape consists of a development, acceptance and production system. In addition, system replication is a requirement for all production systems.

The following SAP HANA landscape has been designed (see Figure 2.3):

▶ There are two appliances; one for the production and another for the non-production SAP HANA systems.

▶ The appliance for production hosts an MDC installation for the production SAP-HANA systems. The MDC consists of a system database and three production databases, one each for SAP ERP, SAP PO and SAP CRM.

▶ The appliance for the non-production systems hosts two MDC installations. One MDC installation for the development and another for acceptance systems. Each MDC installation has one system database and three non-production databases, one each for SAP ERP, SAP PO and SAP CRM. The two MDC installations have their own SID and software installation and are actually MCOS (multiple SAP HANA installations on one system). MCOS is explained in detail in Section 2.1.4.

▶ On the appliance for the non-production systems, there is an MDC installation for the failover of the production MDC system. This SAP HANA system has the same layout as the SAP HANA system on the production system and system replication is set up between both.

▶ Only SAP HANA is installed on the appliances. The SAP application servers for SAP ERP, SAP PO and SAP CRM are installed on two ESX servers running VMware. High availability for the production application servers is guaranteed by VMware HA (see Section 7.1.1).

▶ Finally, each ESX server also hosts an SAP Content Server or MaxDB database.

2.1.3 Multiple Applications on One HANA System (MCOD)

With the Multiple Components in One SAP HANA system (MCOD) setup, several independent SAP components can be installed in one database. Every component uses a different database user schema.

MCOD is not unique to SAP HANA

 MCOD has been around for quite some time. These systems have been mostly used to combine SAP ERP with SAP CRM or SAP SRM systems. SAP CRM and SAP SRM read and write data from and to the backend system SAP ERP. They need the backend system to function correctly. As such, downtime on SAP ERP systems always results in downtime of SAP CRM and SAP SRM, whether they use MCOD or not.

Figure 2.3: SAP HANA landscape with MDC and MCOS

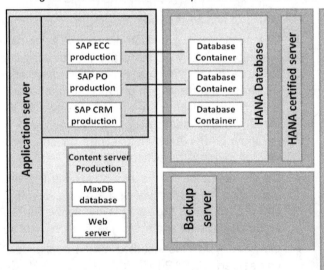

This deployment type is available for production SAP HANA systems, albeit with restrictions. The restrictions are listed in SAP Note 1661202 - Support for multiple applications on SAP HANA. If the Business Suite is deployed on the SAP HANA system, the restrictions of SAP Note 1826100 - Multiple applications SAP Business Suite powered by SAP HANA apply.

Further considerations: there is a section of Note 1661202 that discusses aspects that should be taken into account when considering deploying multiple applications on the same SAP HANA system. Some of the key considerations discussed in this section are as follows:

▶ If running multiple applications on one SAP HANA system, there is a risk that one application could consume a significant amount of available CPU and memory resources, thereby reducing the amount of such resources available for the other applications at a given point in time.

▶ Capacity planning is crucial when combining different applications, components and scenarios on a single SAP HANA system. You must determine the resource allocation needs for each application and then add them together to estimate the required sizing for your SAP HANA system.

▶ Backup and Recovery is only supported at the SAP HANA database level, and not at the database schema level. This means that

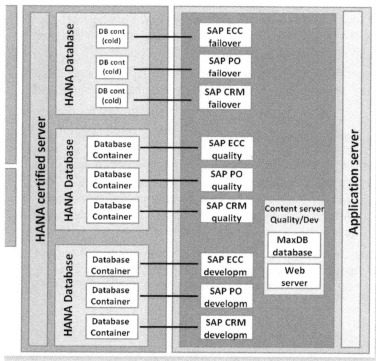

a point-in-time recovery for the SAP HANA system will impact all applications residing on that SAP HANA system. This is unacceptable from a disaster recovery perspective. MCOD should, therefore, only be considered for non-production systems.

▶ A system copy of one application is not possible. The database is always copied completely.

▶ High availability is always done at database level, not at application level.

2.1.4 Multiple applications on One SAP HANA System (MCOS)

Several applications on one System (MCOS) simply refers to the scenario where more than one SAP HANA database is installed on one server.

Each of the databases in this configuration has its own System Identifier (SID), software installation and directory structure. They are basically completely independent from any other database which may reside on the same system.

MCOS is supported with restrictions. These restrictions are documented in SAP Note 1681092 - Multiple SAP HANA databases on one SAP HANA system. It basically comes down to the following:

▶ Running multiple SAP HANA DBMS's (SIDS) on a single production SAP HANA hardware installation is supported for single host or scale-up scenarios only. Scale-out is not supported.

▶ Running multiple SAP HANA DBMSs (SIDs) on a single non-production or scale-out SAP HANA environment is supported without restrictions (DEV, QA, test, production fail-over, etc.).

Further considerations:

▶ When deploying MCOS, it's important to ensure that the system is sized appropriately, with capacity planning that reflects the additional resources necessary to accommodate the additional database(s). SAP recommends working closely with the hardware partner to ensure adequate capacity planning.

▶ Additionally, running MCOS may impact performance of various types of operations, as competition for memory and or CPU resources may occur. This performance impact can occur despite adequate sizing. MCOS is not recommended for use cases where optimal performance is considered particularly important.

Figure 2.4 is an example of an MCOS environment. The production SAP HANA system is isolated on the primary appliance. The development and acceptance SAP HANA systems share the secondary appliance together with the failover SAP HANA system for production. If a system failure occurs on the primary appliance, the production SAP HANA system is resumed on the secondary system and the development and acceptance SAP HANA system are stopped. The primary appliance is a standard SAP HANA deployment or SCOS while the secondary appliance is a typical example of a Several Databases on One System or MCOS.

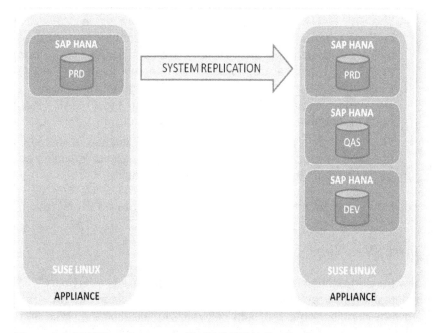

Figure 2.4: MCOS environment with SAP HANA Replication

2.1.5   SAP HANA with Virtualization

With virtualization, each virtual machine houses an independent operating system and appears like a real host. From the SAP HANA server installation perspective, it appears as if the SAP HANA database is deployed in the same manner as the standard SAP HANA deployment.

There are some important restrictions in regard to the technical deployment type SAP HANA with virtualization that must be considered. An important reference for the topic of SAP HANA with virtualization is SAP Note 1788665—SAP HANA running on VMware vSphere VMs and the FAQ document that is attached to that note.

The following considerations should be taken into account with virtualization:

► Each SAP HANA instance or virtual machine needs to be sized according to the existing SAP HANA sizing guidelines and corresponding hypervisor vendor recommendations.

► CPU and memory over-provisioning must not be used.

► The SAP HANA system setup needs to be done by an SAP HANA certified engineer on SAP HANA certified hardware and successfully verified with the SAP HANA hardware configuration check tool (SAP HANA Tailored Datacenter Integration option). Alternatively, the system can be delivered pre-configured with the hypervisor and the SAP HANA software installed by an SAP HANA hardware partner (SAP HANA appliance option).

► The maximum size of a virtual SAP HANA instance is limited by the maximum size the hypervisor supports per virtual machine and the application dependent core-to-memory ratios.

Virtualization comes in two flavors, software and hardware virtualization.

Software Virtualization

Software virtualization is done by software, or so-called hypervisor, which emulates a physical machine. The difference between software and hardware virtualization is that with software virtualization the same hardware platform is shared between the hypervisor and the virtual machine.

Software virtualization on an x86 hardware platform will only be able to run virtual machines capable of running on that platform. The hypervisor divides the hardware resources among the different virtual machines or guests. The biggest advantage of virtualization is that hardware resources can be better divided according to the needs of the different virtual systems. These guest operating systems are unaware of the fact that they are running on a virtualized environment. Examples of software virtualization are VMware and Microsoft Hyper-V.

The following hypervisors are currently supported with SAP HANA:

VMware vSphere

- ▶ VMware vSphere 5.1 with SAP HANA SPS 05 or later for non-production use cases
- ▶ VMware vSphere 5.5 with SAP HANA SPS 07 or later for production and non-production use cases:
  - ▶ in general availability for single-VM scenarios (See SAP Note 1995460 for specific information and constraints).
  - ▶ in general availability for multi-VM scenarios (See SAP Note 2024433 for specific information and constraints).
  - ▶ in general availability for SAP BW, powered by SAP HANA scale-out scenarios (See SAP Note 2157587 for specific information and constraints).
- ▶ VMware vSphere 6.0
  - ▶ in general availability for SAP HANA SPS 09 or later for non-production use cases
  - ▶ in general availability for and with SAP HANA SPS 11 or later for production single-VM scenarios (See SAP Note 2315348 for specific information and constraints).

Hitachi LPAR 2.0

Hitachi LPAR 2.0 is supported as of SAP HANA SPS 07 for production and non-production use cases. It is in controlled availability for single and multi-VM scenarios. (See SAP Note 2063057 for specific information and constraints).

IBM PowerVM

IBM Power VM LPAR on IBM Power Systems is supported for production use-cases. It is generally available for single-VM and multi-VM scenarios with up to 4 LPARs on 1 server. (See SAP Note 2055470 for specific information and constraints).

KVM and XEN

Software virtualization with KVM (on SUSE SLES 11 and 12 or Redhat RHEL 7.x) and XEN (on SUSE SLES 11 and 12) with SAP HANA SPS 11 (or later releases) are supported for non-production use cases.

Huawei FusionSphere

Software virtualization is supported with Huawei FusionSphere version 3.1 and 5.1:

▶ support for FusionSphere 3.1 as of SAP HANA SPS 09 for production and non-production use cases in controlled availability for single-VM scenarios (See SAP Note 2186187 for specific information and constraints).

▶ support for FusionSphere 5.1 as of SAP HANA SPS 10 / 11 for production and non-production use cases in controlled availability for single-VM, multi-VM and scale-out scenarios (See SAP Note 2279020 for specific information and constraints).

Be aware that access to these SAP Notes is restricted to customers participating in the controlled availability phase.

Hardware Virtualization

With hardware-enabled virtualization or partitioning, the software which divides the hardware among the different partitions is implemented in the hardware itself. The partitions are electrically isolated. They operate independently of each other, even to the extent that a partition can be powered up or down without impacting any of the other partitions. An advantage of hardware partitioning is that there is no software hypervisor and, therefore, less overhead for the virtualization layer.

Hardware partitioning technology currently supported for running SAP HANA in a partitioned environment are:

Hewlett Packard nPartitions

▶ HP nPartitions in the context of HP CS 900 with Superdome X servers for production and non-production use cases. (See SAP Note 2103848 for more specific information and constraints).

Fujitsu Physical Partitioning

▶ Fujitsu physical partitioning with PRIMEQUEST 2400 E/L and PRIMEQUEST 2800 E/L for production and non-production use cases. (See SAP Note 2111714 for more specific information and constraints).

Lenovo FlexNode

▶ Lenovo FlexNode partitions in the context of Lenovo x3950 X6 servers for production and non-production use cases. (See SAP Note 2232700 for more specific information and constraints).

2.1.6 Deployment Options Compared

Table 2.1 compares the different deployment options together with their advantages and disadvantages.

Feature	SCOS	MDC	MCOD	MCOS	HW level Virtualization	SW Level Virtualization
Production support?	Yes	Yes	With restrictions	Scale-up only	Yes	With restrictions
Shared resources (performance)?	No	Yes	Yes	Yes	Yes	Yes
Shared SAP HANA installation?	No	Yes	Yes	No	No	No
Shared backup / recovery	No	No	Yes	No	No	No
High availability	System or storage replication	System or storage replication	System or storage replication	System or storage replication	System or storage replication	System or storage replication HA on the virtualization layer
License	SAP HANA	SAP HANA	SAP HANA	SAP HANA	SAP HANA	SAP HANA virtualization license

Table 2.1: Comparison—SAP HANA deployment options

To summarize, the following deployment options exist:

The single application option

There are no limitations with the standard option, but since hardware is not shared it is the most expensive option.

Multitenant database containers

Multitenant database containers allow a combination of multiple databases on the same hardware with few limitations. The most important being the shared SAP HANA software release.

SAP considers the multitenant database containers the standard deployment option for SAP HANA.

Multiple applications in one SAP HANA system

Multiple Components in One SAP HANA system (MCOD) is an older alternative for operating multiple production systems on the same hardware. MCOD should not be considered. The showstopper is backup and recovery. Backup and recovery is currently supported only at the SAP HANA database level and not at the database schema level. This means that a point-in-time recovery for the SAP HANA system will impact all applications residing on that SAP HANA system. This is unacceptable from a disaster recovery perspective.

Multiple applications on one HANA system

Multiple Components on one System (MCOS) is an option to have different SAP HANA systems on the same hardware. It is useful when hardware is used by multiple independent systems. An often-seen layout is an MCOS system in which the disaster recovery production is installed on the same system as the acceptance or development system.

SAP HANA with Virtualization

Virtualization provides good control of physical resources and is, therefore, quite flexible. In our opinion, virtualization only makes sense when shared storage is available. As such, it should be considered in combination with the SAP HANA Tailored Datacenter Integration (TDI) installation option.

Different deployment options can be combined. A layout often used is the Multitenant Database Containers (MDC) combined with Several Databases on One System (MCOS) option. An MDC is set up for the production SAP HANA databases on one SAP HANA appliance and several MDC SAP HANA systems are set up for the non-production SAP HANA databases on another SAP HANA appliance (for example, one MDC for development and another for acceptance). As such, the SAP HANA appliance for the non-production systems is actually Several Databases on One System (MCOS).

2.1.7   Multitenant Database Containers versus Virtualization

A Multitenant Database Container (MDC) SAP HANA system combines multiple databases in a single SAP HANA instance. These databases are referred to as multitenant database containers. Apart from sharing the same instance, they are completely isolated from one another. MDC is therefore often considered a sort of virtualization.

There are however some crucial differences:

► TCO is lower than with virtualization as there is a single software stack. There is no need for a virtualization or additional operating system license.

► All databases share the same instance. An upgrade of the SAP HANA revision impacts all tenants. This is not the case with virtualization because every SAP HANA system is isolated on a dedicated virtual machine.

► MDC has a performance advantage over standard virtualization as there is no overhead of the Hypervisor.

Table 2.2 compares the differences between MDC and virtualization.

Feature	MDC	HW level Virtualization	SW Level Virtualization
Production support?	Yes	Yes	Yes
Performance overhead	Low	Medium	High (compared to MDC)
Resource management	SAP HANA	Firmware	Hypervisor
Workload isolation	SAP HANA	OS Level	OS Level
Shared SAP HANA installation?	Yes	No	No
HW vendor independent	Yes	No	Yes
Max. Instance	Unlimited	HW vendor limit	Hypervisor limit
License	SAP HANA	No	Yes

Table 2.2: MDC versus virtualization

2.2 SAP HANA and the SAP Application Server on one system

So far, we have only talked about the SAP HANA system. One could almost forget that in addition to the SAP HANA system there is still the SAP NetWeaver ABAP or JAVA application server to host somewhere.

For existing SAP customers, the SAP application server remains on the already existing hardware during the migration or upgrade to SAP HANA. It is only the database which is migrated. A customer running on Windows with Oracle still runs the SAP application server on Windows after the migration to SAP HANA.

Thus, the migration to SAP HANA is, for many customers, a migration to a distributed environment in which the SAP application server is running on another hardware system than the SAP HANA system.

As of SAP HANA SP07, SAP supports the option to install an SAP NetWeaver application server on the SAP HANA hardware (see Figure 2.5).

This gives you the following options:

▶ The Central Services Instance (ASCS) and the Primary Application Server (PAS) on the same hardware as the SAP HANA system.

▶ The first option but in a High-Availability layout using clustering software with system replication between the primary and secondary SAP HANA system. In addition, an Enqueue Replication Server (ERS) is installed on the secondary system, connected to the Enqueue Service of the Central Services Instance (ASCS). Using cluster software, the ASCS and Primary Application Server can fail over to the secondary system. The SAP HANA system is protected by system replication. If the primary fails, the secondary SAP HANA system takes over.

These scenarios are explained in detail in SAP Notes 1953429 (AS ABAP) and 2043509 (AS Java).

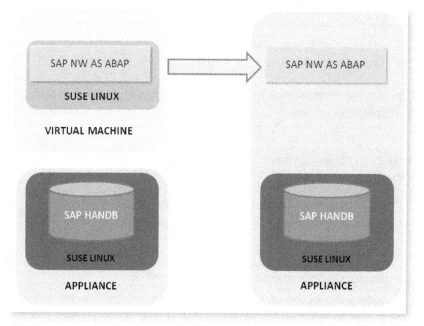

Figure 2.5: SAP HANA and the SAP Application Server

2.3　Data Provisioning

In the SAP HANA as Data Mart or Accelerator scenario, an SAP HANA database is initially empty. In-memory reporting and analyzing of business data requires that data be copied from the traditional applications to SAP HANA.

This is done using a replication scenario. The following components are involved in all replication scenarios:

▶ the SAP HANA database

▶ the SAP or non-SAP source system

▶ software components supporting the data replication such as the SAP Landscape Transformation Replication Server (SLT)

Different tools exist for different replication scenarios (see Figure 2.6):

▶ SAP Landscape Transformation Replication Server

▶ SAP Replication Server

▶ SAP Data Services

▶ SAP Event Stream Processor

▶ SAP MobiLink

▶ Direct Extractor Connection

▶ Smart Data Access

All of the above tools, except Smart Data Access, do data replication. The difference is in the replication methodology and the source system type.

The following checklist can be used when selecting a replication scenario and corresponding solution:

▶ Is the source system an SAP or non-SAP system?

▶ Is the source system a relational database management system (RDBMS)?

▶ Is real-time replication needed or is near real-time or batch based replication acceptable?

▶ Is data replication needed from electronic devices?

▶ Is data access instead of data replication acceptable?

Data Provisioning for SAP HANA

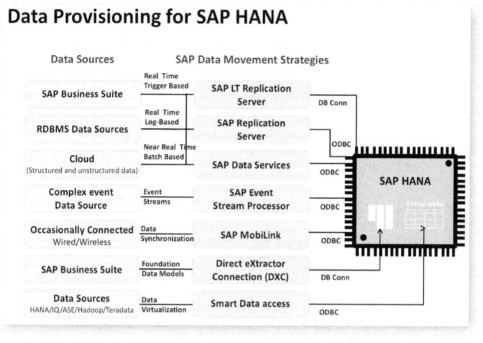

Figure 2.6: Data Provisioning for SAP HANA

2.3.1 SAP Landscape Transformation Replication Server

The SAP Landscape Transformation Replication Server (SLT) is the SAP technology that allows you to load and replicate data in real time from ABAP source systems and non-ABAP source systems to an SAP HANA environment. SAP LT uses the same technology as the SAP Test Data Migration Server (TDMS) by delivering a trigger-based replication approach to pass data from the source system to the target system.

Landscape Overview

This replication method requires the following components:

▶ SAP ERP system (source)—The source system tracks database changes by using database triggers. It records information about changes in the logging tables. Read modules (located on the ABAP source system) transfer the data from the source system to the SAP LT Replication Server. The relevant data is read from the application tables.

- ▶ SAP Landscape Transformation Replication server—The SLT server controls the entire replication process by triggering the initial load and coordinating the delta replication. Technically, the SLT is an add-on that can be installed on any NetWeaver system. This can be installed on the SAP ERP system itself (embedded) or on a standalone SAP system.

- ▶ The SAP HANA system contains the SAP HANA database. It is used to store the replicated data. The SAP LT Replication Server and the SAP HANA system communicate by means of a database connection.

Embedded versus standalone installation

The SAP LT Replication Server can be installed either as a separate SAP system or, if the technical prerequisites permit, on an ABAP source system. Configuration of data replication is done on the SAP LT Replication Server.

Table 2.3 compares the embedded with the standalone installation option, with their advantages and disadvantages.

	Embedded	Dedicated
Advantages	Simplified administration	Performance isolated on dedicated system No software dependencies
Disadvantages	Performance impact on backend Software dependencies	Extra SAP landscape needed
Requirements	Non-Unicode is not supported	New installation is per default Unicode

Table 2.3: Advantages and disadvantages of an embedded or dedicated system

The SAP LT Replication Server uses background processing to replicate data. This may have a significant impact on performance. It is, therefore, recommended to install the SAP LT replication on a dedicated SAP NetWeaver system.

This results in an increase in the number of systems in the SAP landscape because for every development, acceptance and production SAP

ERP system, there is a need for an SAP LT Replication Server. Figure 2.7 is an example of such an SAP landscape.

SAP Landscape Transformation Server needs Unicode

The SAP Landscape Transformation Server needs to be installed on a Unicode system. If your backend system is still non-Unicode, the dedicated or standalone installation option is the only option.

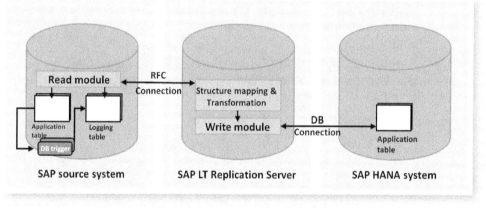

Figure 2.7: SAP SLT on a dedicated SAP NetWeaver system

SAP landscapes with SAP SLT on dedicated SAP NetWeaver systems tend to be big as the SAP SLT layout needs to be copied through the full SAP landscape to support development, quality assurance and production.

Consider the following example of an SAP landscape. The customer has two SAP BW landscapes; each SAP BW landscape consists of a development, acceptance and production system. SAP HANA will also be used for the SAP FICO accelerator. In addition, system replication is a requirement for both SAP BW production systems.

The following SAP HANA landscape has been designed (see Figure 2.8):

▶ There are two appliances, one for the production and another for the non-production SAP HANA systems.

▶ The appliance for production hosts an MDC installation for the production SAP-HANA systems. The MDC consists of two SAP

BW production databases and a database for the SAP FICO accelerator.

▶ The appliance for the non-production systems hosts two MDC installations. One MDC installation for the development and another for acceptance systems. Each MDC installation has two SAP BW databases and a database for the SAP FICO accelerator. The two MDC installations have their own SID and software installation and are actually MCOS (multiple SAP HANA installations on one system).

▶ On the appliance for the non-production systems, there is an MDC installation for the failover of the production MDC system This SAP HANA system has the same layout as the SAP HANA system on the production system, and system replication is set up between both.

▶ SAP SLT on dedicated SAP NetWeaver systems. As the SAP system layout needs to be synchronized between the development, acceptance and production systems, there are three SAP SLT systems.

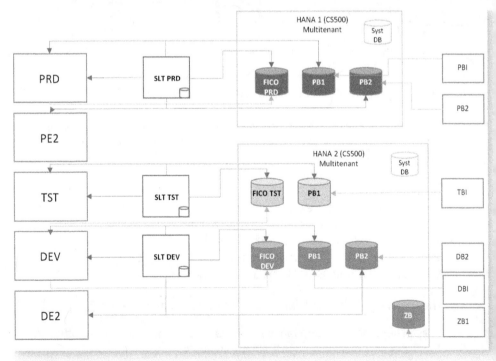

Figure 2.8: SAP Landscape with SAP SLT and SAP HANA MDC and MCOS system layouts.

2.3.2 SAP Replication Server

Transaction Log-Based Data Replication is based on capturing table changes from low-level database log files.

SAP Replication Server (SRS) supports log-based replication from and to different databases. You can use SAP Replication Server to do an initial load as well as replication in real time. Replication can be done at both table and database level.

The following source databases are supported:

▶ Sybase ASE
▶ Oracle
▶ Microsoft SQL Server
▶ DB2 UDB LUW
▶ SAP HANA database

For these databases, initial load and continuous replication configuration can be done without any downtime on the primary database.

2.3.3 SAP Data Services

Extraction-Transformation and Load (ETL) based data replication is a service of SAP Data Services, which is part of the Business Objects portfolio. It is used to extract, transform and load business data from SAP and non-SAP sources to the SAP HANA database. SAP Data Services is also capable of reading data files such as comma delimited, fixed width, COBOL, XML, and many more.

ETL consists of data flows and replication jobs, and permits data checks, transformations, synchronization with additional data providers, and data merging. SAP Data Services loads data at specific intervals and features complex transformations of data while transferring.

The main components of Data Services are the Data Services Designer, where data flows are modeled, and the Data Services Job Server for the execution of the replication jobs. An additional repository is used on the Data Services server to store the metadata and the job definitions.

2.3.4 SAP Smart Data Streaming

SAP HANA Smart Data Streaming is an option of SAP HANA used to process streams of incoming event data in real time and act on them immediately. Some examples of data sources that produce streams of events in real time include:

- ▶ equipment sensors to measure temperature or humidity levels
- ▶ smart devices
- ▶ web sites (click streams)
- ▶ IT systems (logs)
- ▶ financial markets (prices)
- ▶ social media

Data is collected through adapters or sensors which connect to the smart data-streaming server. The streaming server contains business logic which is immediately applied to the incoming data, only capturing the data actually needed. Raw data can be filtered and alerts sent to other applications or streamed to live dashboards.

SAP Smart Data Streaming and The Internet of Things

 Everybody is talking about the Internet of Things these days. But what is it all about? Simply put, the Internet of Things is a concept of connecting any electronic device to the Internet. This applies not only to computers, smartphones, and tablets, but also to your television and air-conditioning, and even to the engine of your car. These devices generate an enormous amount of data, which can be analyzed, for example, to improve the fuel consumption of cars. With SAP Smart Data Streaming, you can capture the incoming data, filter and transform it. You can actively monitor data arriving from sensors and smart devices, and set alerts to be triggered when immediate attention is required, for example, if an engine of an airplane is triggering too many alerts.

70

2.3.5 SAP Mobilink

SAP Mobilink is a synchronization technology designed to synchronize UltraLite and SAP SQL Anywhere remote databases with a consolidated database.

What is UltraLite?

 UltraLite is an RDMBS designed to use a minimum amount of memory and storage resources. It is ideal for iPhone, Android and Windows Mobile applications. It is transaction-based, like any other RDMBS and has built-in synchronization technology to exchange data with other databases.

What about SAP SQL Anywhere?

 SAP SQL Anywhere is software which includes an RDMBS, data exchanges and synchronization technology. It is available for server, desktops and mobile devices.

SAP Mobilink can be used to connect devices which only connect occasionally. This implies that data needs to be saved on the device and synchronized with the central database when a connection is made.

With SAP MobiLink events are stored locally on the device and synchronized at regular intervals, whereas with SAP Smart Data Streaming, data is constantly sent to the central database.

2.3.6 Direct Extractor Connection

The SAP Landscape Transformation Server is applicable when data needs to be copied and converted to the SAP HANA system in real time. For business cases in which interval replication is acceptable, the Direct Extract Connection (DXC) is a valid alternative. DXC uses the SAP Business Content to guarantee data integrity.

SAP Business Content DataSource Extractors have been available in the SAP BW system for many years and are the basis for data modeling and data acquisition. With the SAP HANA Direct Extractor Connection (DXC), these SAP Business Content DataSource Extractors are available to deliver data directly to SAP HANA.

DXC is a data acquisition technique; it should be considered as a form of extraction, transformation and load although its transformation capabilities are limited to user exit for extraction.

DCX is batch-driven and is applicable if interval replication is acceptable (for example, every 15 minutes).

The pre-configured data models for use in SAP HANA data mart scenarios bring the following added values:

▶ significantly reduce complexity of data modeling tasks

▶ reduce the implementation time of the project

▶ ensure data consistency and application logic

In addition, the Direct Extractor Connection reduces Total Cost of Ownership (TCO) by:

▶ reusing existing extraction, transformation, and load mechanism built into the SAP systems over a simple http(s) connection to SAP HANA

▶ eliminating the need for an additional server or application in system landscape

▶ reducing data transfer by only copying changed data into SAP HANA

DXC for SAP Business Suite

 As of SAP NetWeaver version 7.0, SAP Business Warehouse (BW) is part of SAP NetWeaver itself, which means that a BW system exists inside every SAP component running on NetWeaver such as SAP ERP or SAP CRM. This embedded BW system inside SAP Business Suite systems is actually not utilized by many SAP customers. Instead, they run SAP BW on a separate server. By default, DXC utilizes the scheduling and monitoring features of the embedded BW system. Data is not stored locally, nor is any reporting functionality used. DXC extraction processing essentially bypasses the normal dataflow and instead sends data to SAP HANA.

2.3.7 Smart Data Access

SAP HANA Smart Data Access enables remote data or tables to be accessed as if they were local tables in SAP HANA, without copying the data into SAP HANA, by using virtual tables. The virtual tables point to the remote tables in the remote databases. SQL statements can work with these virtual tables as if they were local tables. Analytical applications can benefit from this capability as data can be accessed and integrated from multiple systems in real time regardless of where the data is located or what systems are generating it.

The following remote data sources are supported:

► SAP HANA
► SAP IQ
► SAP Adaptive Server Enterprise
► SAP Event Stream Processor
► SAP MaxDB
► Apache Hadoop
► Teradata Database
► Microsoft SQL Server 2012
► Oracle Database 12C
► IBM DB2
► IBM Netezza Appliance
► Apache Spark

3 Scalability

With SAP-HANA, scalability is translated to scale-up and scale-out (see Figure 3.1). Scale-up is straightforward—add capacity! Increase memory, CPU and storage as needed or up the hardware limit of the SAP HANA appliance. If the hardware limit is reached, move your SAP HANA to a new, larger appliance.

Scale-up is currently limited to 12 TB of memory but this limit will probably already have been exceeded by the time you read this book.

Please note that the scale-up server hardware for OLAP applications, such as SAP Business Warehouse, differs from server hardware for OLTP applications, such as SAP Business Suite powered by SAP HANA products. The amount of memory is always related to the amount of CPU cores. For OLTP applications, more RAM per CPU core is possible.

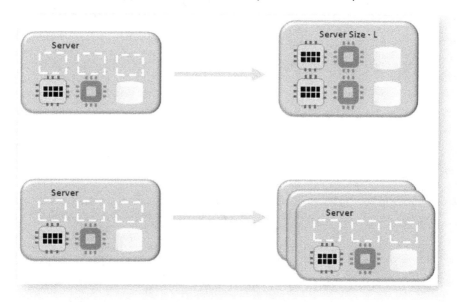

Figure 3.1: Scale-up versus Scale-out

3.1 Scale-Out

A scale-out SAP HANA system consists of separate SAP HANA servers or nodes linked together. Data is distributed across the nodes and each node takes care of the data processing. An advantage of scale-out is built-in high availability. One or several nodes can be configured as standby. If one of the nodes fails, the standby will take over the data of the failed node and continue processing. As soon as the failed node is available again, it can be re-integrated into the system layout as standby.

Table 3.1 compares scale-up with scale-out and their advantages and disadvantages.

	Scale-up	Scale-out
Support	Every SAP component supported on SAP HANA is supported in a scale-up layout	Limited (see SAP Note 1825774 for detailed information)
Consolidation	Multiple SAP HANA databases can be consolidated on a single SAP-HANA system	Only one SAP-HANA database per system
Complexity	Simple and straightforward	Complex because cross-node communication and data distribution comes into play
Cost	Depends on the resource requirements. The higher the requirements, the higher the cost	Several smaller appliances might be less expensive but maintenance cost might be more expensive
Skills	Limited as a Scale-up solution does not provide table and load distribution, or hash algorithms	SAP HANA knowledge is needed to properly distribute data among the different nodes
Growth	Limited to the capacity of the appliance	Nearly unlimited as nodes can be added as needed
High-Availability	SAP HANA system replication or via shared storage using 1 worker + 1 standby configuration	Scale-out has built-in HA capabilities through the use of one or more standby nodes

Table 3.1: Scale-up versus Scale-out

Larger, single HANA systems (scale-up) are more expensive, but are easier to manage than scale-out systems with distributed data and multiple nodes. Online transaction processing (OLTP) applications such as ERP and CRM are only supported on scale-out SAP HANA systems in specific scenarios and in close cooperation with SAP.

3.2 Scale-Out and High Availability

As scale-out means distributing over multiple machines to create a distributed SAP HANA system, fault-tolerance can be built into the system design. Host auto-failover is a feature which is available for distributed systems. One or more standby hosts are added to distribute installation, and are configured to work in standby mode. As long as they are in standby mode, they do not contain any data and do not accept requests or queries.

When a host fails, a standby host automatically takes its place. Since the standby host may take over operation from any host, it needs shared access to all the database volumes. A shared, networked storage server can accomplish this by using a distributed file system or, with vendor-specific solutions that use the SAP HANA programmatic interface, the Storage Connector API to dynamically detach and attach (mount) networked storage upon failover.

This scenario is illustrated in the graphic below (see Figure 3.2):

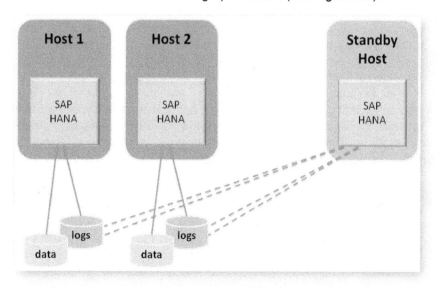

Figure 3.2: Host fail-over in a distributed scenario

Once repaired, the failed host can rejoin the system as the new standby host to reestablish the failure recovery capability.

In support of host auto-failover, applications can be configured with the connection information of multiple hosts, optionally including the standby host. The application will try to connect to one of the hosts. This ensures that applications can continue to reach the SAP HANA database, even after failover.

3.3 Scale-Out and Data Partitioning

The main reason for scale-out or distributing the SAP HANA database across multiple servers is to overcome the hardware limitations of a single physical server. A secondary advantage is that an SAP HANA system can distribute the load between multiple servers by using data or table partitioning. Tables can be assigned to hosts (database partitioning) or split between hosts (table partitioning).

With database partitioning, user schemas and single tables can be assigned to a single host, while others are assigned to different hosts. When a single table is larger than a single server's memory, it can be partitioned among several different servers with table partitioning. Very large tables can be broken up into smaller pieces and distributed among different machines. Table partitioning is transparent for SQL queries and data manipulation language (DML) statements. Additional DDL statements exist for table partitioning itself

The table-partitioning feature of the SAP HANA database splits column-store tables horizontally into partitions or sub-tables. As such, large tables can be broken down into smaller, more manageable parts. Partitioning is used in scale-out systems, but it may also be beneficial in single-host systems. There are several methodologies to partition a table such as hash partitioning or partitioning by range.

SAP HANA scale-out installations

 Partitioning is typically used in scale-out or distributed SAP landscapes

Column-store tables only

Partitioning is only available for column-store tables!

Partitioning has the following advantages:

- ▶ Load balancing and parallelization—As table partitions are distributed among several servers, table queries are processed on all servers that host partitions of that table.

- ▶ Overcoming the size limitation of column-store tables—A table cannot store more than 2 billion rows. Table partitioning can be used to overcome this limit. As partitions are tables themselves, each partition again cannot contain more than 2 billion rows. Fortunately, partitioning can be re-distributed if the size limit looks like it will be reached.

- ▶ Query isolation—If a query only needs a subset of the data, only the partition containing the data will be queried. By doing so, the overall load on the system is reduced and response time improved. For example, if a table is partitioned by year, a query restricted to the data of one year is executed only on the partition with data for that year.

- ▶ Explicit partition handling—The application may drop and create partitions as needed; for example, they can create an extra partition to automatically store sales data for the upcoming quarter.

- ▶ Improvement in the Delta Merge operation—The performance of the delta merge operation depends on the size of the main index. If data is only being modified on some partitions, fewer partitions will need to be delta merged and, therefore, performance will be better.

What is the Delta Merge?

A column store table consists of two indexes; for each column there is a main index and a delta index.

The main index or storage is optimized for read performance and compressed to reduce the memory footprint. The delta storage is optimized for write operations. Using delta storage addresses performance issues which might occur when loading changed data directly to the main storage with its compressed columns.

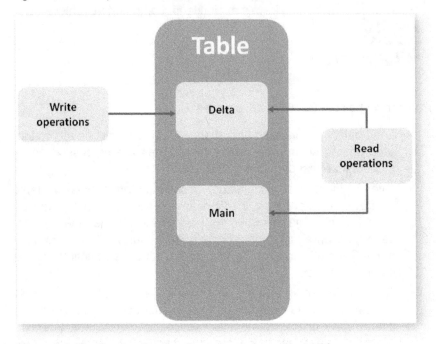

Figure 3.3: Read and write operations on a column store table

Read operations are performed on both parts, whereas update operations only affect the delta part (see Figure 3.3). At some point, the main and delta storage need to be merged; this process is called the delta merge.

3.3.1 Single Level Partitioning

During table partitioning, table data is divided among the different partitions according to different criteria or partitioning specifications. Table partitioning can be done single or multi-level.

The SAP HANA database supports the following single-level partitioning specifications:

- ► Hash
- ► Range
- ► Round-robin

Hash partitioning

Hash partitioning is straightforward and no in-depth knowledge of the content of the data is needed. Rows are distributed equally among the different partitions for load balancing and to overcome the 2-billion-row limitation. A hash function is used to the value of the specified column or columns to assign the partition. The engine determines the number of partitions at runtime. If the table has a primary key, the columns must be part of the key.

Round-robin

Round-robin partitioning is used to achieve an equal distribution of rows to partitions. However, unlike hash partitioning, no partitioning columns need to be specified. Round-robin partitioning assigns rows to partitions on a rotation basis.

Hash partitioning is usually more beneficial than Round-robin partitioning. With Round-robin, data is distributed among all servers. As such, all of them need to be considered in queries and database operations. This is not the case with Hash partitioning.

Range partitioning

Range partitioning creates dedicated partitions for certain values or value ranges in a table. Knowledge of the data content is needed. For example, a range partitioning scheme can be chosen to create a partition for each calendar month. An advantage of range partitioning is that applications can manage the partitions themselves. An application can decide to drop a partition containing data from 48 months ago and create a new one for the upcoming month so that new data is inserted into that new partition.

Range partitioning is similar to Hash partitioning in that the partitioning column must be part of the primary key. Range partitioning is also restricted in terms of the data types that can be used.

Range partitioning is not well suited to load distribution. It is restricted to the data types that can be used and tends to create hot spots. If, for example, partitions are created on a quarterly basis, new data will be inserted solely in the last created partition, resulting in a potential performance bottleneck.

3.3.2 Multi Level Partitioning

Hash and Range partitioning have the limitation that only the key columns can be used as partitioning columns.

Multi-level partitioning can be used to overcome this limitation as it makes it possible to partition by a column that is not part of the primary key. Multi-level partitioning is a time-based partitioning specification. For some tables, it is beneficial to partition by a date column which is not part of the primary key; for example, if a data column is present and it is desirable to leverage it in order to build partitions per month or year. With multi-level partitioning, the key columns need to be used in the first level; the second level can be used for determining the time creation.

Multi-Level partitioning is a combination of the Single-Level partitioning specifications:

▶ Hash-Range: Hash on the first level, Range partitioning on the second to determine the time criterion. Figure 3.4 shows a typical usage scenario; the load is distributed via a Hash partitioning to three server nodes. A Range partitioning on the second level distributes the data to individual partitions per month.

▶ Round-robin Hash: Round-robin first and Hash partitioning on the second level.

▶ Hash-Hash: Two-level partitioning with Hash on both levels. The advantage is that the Hash on the second level may be defined on a non-key column.

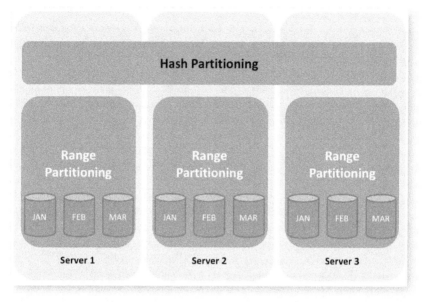

Figure 3.4: Hash-Range partitioning

Multi-level partitioning— it's all about performance

 The performance of the delta merge is dependent on the size of the table. Multi-level partitioning can increase performance for time or data-based data. Old data is rarely modified and as such no delta merges are needed on these partitions. The delta merges are only required on new partitions in which data is inserted. The smaller the partitions, the faster the delta merges. Multi-level partitioning allows you to keep the partitions equal in size and therefore performance remains constant, while new partitions are being created and used.

4 Disaster Recovery

Although SAP HANA is an in-memory database, it saves all changes to data such as row insertions, deletions and updates to disk. This ensures that it can resume from a system shutdown or power-failure without loss of data. Data persistence by itself is, however, not sufficient from a disaster recovery perspective. In this chapter, we discuss the storage concepts of SAP HANA and the available backup and recovery options.

SAP HANA is an in-memory database.

So, what happens when the power goes down?

To maintain optimal performance, the SAP HANA database holds the bulk of its data in memory. So what happens when the power goes down or when the system fails? Luckily, SAP HANA uses storage to provide a fallback in the event of a failure. During normal database operation, changed data is automatically saved from memory to disk at regular save points. Additionally, all data changes are recorded in the redo log buffer. When a database transaction is committed, the redo log buffer is saved to disk. If the redo log buffer fills at any time, the redo log buffer is saved to disk, even if no commit has been sent, just as any traditional database would.

When the system fails or when the database needs to be restarted for maintenance, the database is started in the same way as any disk-based database and is returned to its last consistent state by replaying the redo log since the last save point.

Data persistence is, however, not sufficient from a disaster recovery point of view as the database remains unprotected from natural disasters, human mistakes and system failures.

Fortunately, with SAP HANA, database online backups of data and logs or storage snapshots are possible.

4.1   What is Disaster Recovery?

This paragraph is an introduction to disaster recovery planning (DRP). It explains the basic concept, the difference between Recovery Point and Recovery Time Objective, the differences between planned and un-planned downtime, and introduces how to protect your SAP landscape from the latter.

Disaster recovery is a methodology which consists of a set of procedures and best-practices to enable the recovery or continuation of the datacenter, systems, databases and applications following a disaster. There are two types of disasters, natural or human-caused disasters. The first category is natural disasters such as floods, hurricanes, tornadoes or earthquakes. The second category is human-caused disasters such as infrastructure failure, failed implementation projects or, basically, human mistakes. Protecting against a natural disaster is complicated, but possible. Areas in which floods, tornadoes or earthquakes often take place are well known. Building your data center next to a volcano might not be a good option. For the second category, human-caused disasters, change management is a must-have. Disaster recovery focuses on the systems and applications supporting critical business functions.

Protecting your business should not be limited to the IT infrastructure. The Disaster Recovery procedures should be part of your company's Business Continuity program. Business Continuity involves keeping all essential aspects of a business functioning despite a disruptive event. Business Continuity goes much further than Disaster Recovery. Disaster Recovery focuses on IT operations whereas Business Continuity considers critical business processes. Consider this example: there is no advantage in having your systems and applications available within two hours if, due to a fire, the factory needs to be rebuilt from scratch. Business continuity should consider the Business Process from start to finish.

Disaster recovery was developed in the mid to late 1970s as computer systems became more and more powerful and organizations became more and more dependent on them being continually available. Data center managers began to realize that something had to be done. Although at that time most systems were batch-oriented mainframes which, in many cases, could be down for a number of days before significant damage could be done to the organization, computer systems in those days were not all as available as they are today and, as such, replacing them could easily have taken days.

4.2 Recovery Point Objective versus Recovery Time Objective

Prior to selecting a Disaster Recovery strategy, a Business Continuity plan should be set up. The Business Continuity plan should indicate the Recovery Point Objective (RPO) and Recovery Time Objective (RTO) for various business processes (such as processes to run payroll, generate an order, etc.). These numbers, specified per business process, are then mapped to the underlying applications, databases and systems supporting those processes.

The setting up of disaster recovery procedures is not a solely technical endeavor. It is up to management and key business users to define the Recovery Point Objective (RPO) and Recovery Time Objective (RTO). Once these are clearly set, the technical solutions have to be implemented to match those requirements.

A Recovery Point Objective (RPO) is the maximum-targeted period in which data might be lost due to a major incident. The RPO gives systems designers a limit to work to. For instance, if the RPO is set to four hours, a maximum of four hours of data may be lost. In practice, a daily off-site backup on tape will not suffice. Solutions such as database mirroring or data replication need to be considered.

A Recovery Time Objective (RTO) is the targeted duration of time within which a system must again be available after a failure occurs in order to avoid unacceptable consequences. For example, if the RTO is set to four hours, then, in practice, the production system must be up and running within four hours after the interruption.

It is up to management to decide if the RPO and RTO includes the time to try to fix the problem; the recovery itself; user acceptance testing; the communication to the end-users; and the reactivaton of all interfaces.

The relation and difference between the RPO and RTO is shown in Figure 4.1.

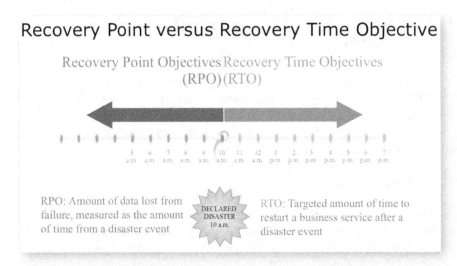

Figure 4.1: Recovery Point Objective versus Recovery Time Objective

In our experience, the Recovery Point Objective is more important than the Recovery Time Objective. Losing business data is unacceptable. Reconstructing the last hours of lost data is extremely time-consuming, expensive and, in many cases, impossible. Going back to the user community after a disaster and asking them to redo what they did over the last few hours is unworkable. What if somebody asked you to redo what you had done in the previous hour, in exactly the same sequence as you had done before? I bet that you couldn't! In the case of automated warehouses, it is actually technically impossible. If the RPO cannot be met due to unforeseeable issues, management will probably accept that the RTO is also not met and will allow more time for IT to recover to the required RPO. Note that the setting up of a proper disaster recovery procedure is done specifically to avoid this.

Many technical solutions exist to deal with natural and human-caused disasters and to meet the Recovery Point and Recovery Time Objectives. In most situations the solution or combination of solutions implemented is a trade-off between maximum protection and cost. Because, make no mistake, disaster recovery solutions are expensive, very expensive.

4.3   Concepts

The key to SAP HANA's performance is keeping as much data as possible in memory. However, SAP HANA also uses persistent storage to provide a fallback in the event of a failure. During normal database operation, changed data is automatically saved from memory to disk at regular save points, just as any other traditional database does. By default, save points are set to occur every five minutes. Data changes are recorded in the redo log buffer. When a database transaction is committed, the redo log buffer is saved to disk. In addition, if the redo log buffer fills at any time, the redo log buffer is saved to disk anyway, even if no commit has been sent.

If a failure occurs, the database can be restarted in the same way as any traditional database. When SAP HANA is restarted, it immediately performs an online-recovery and returns to the last consistent state before shutdown.

Disk persistence is not sufficient from a disaster recovery perspective because it does not protect against system failures, natural disasters or human mistakes. Proper backup and recovery procedures need to be put in place.

SAP HANA has the following features when it comes to backup and recovery:

▶ Backups are always made online. As such, while data backups, log backups and storage snapshots are being created, the database remains available for end users.

▶ Data and log backups are performed independently of each other.

4.3.1 Database Backup

There are two types of database backups: complete and delta. A delta backup can be differential or incremental. A differential backup saves all data changed since the last full backup. An incremental backup saves all data changed since the last full, differential or incremental backup.

Complete Data Backup

A database backup includes all the content of the database. With a database backup, only the actual data is backed up; unused or free space in the database is not backed up. If SAP HANA is running in a scale-out setup, the data backup includes all specific backup parts for all hosts.

An integrity check is performed while the backup is running. Only if the check is successful is the data written to the backup destination.

Delta Backup

Delta backups only back up changed data since the last full or last delta backup. They allow you to reduce the amount of data that is backed up compared to full data backups. Delta backups are not only faster to create than full data backups, they are also smaller.

SAP HANA supports the two types of delta backups: differential backups and incremental backups (see Table 4.1).

	Differential Backup	Incremental Backup
Details	Saves all the data changed since the last full data backup	Saves the data changed since the last full data backup or the last delta backup (incremental or differential)
Backup	The amount of data to be saved with each differential backup increases as the amount of changed data increases since the full backup	Only changed data is backed up; Incremental backups are the smallest of the backup types
Recovery	Only two backups are needed for a recovery—the full data backup and the last differential backup	The full data backup on which the incremental backups are based and each incremental backup made since the full data backup are needed

Table 4.1: Differential versus incremental backups

Database restore always starts from a full backup, followed by the delta backups, if any. A restore with delta backups is always faster than restoring with log backups as only the changed data is recovered, whereas with log backups, each log entry needs to be processed separately before it is recovered. Every recorded transaction is re-executed. Processing multiple log backups is normally more intensive than recovering a small number of delta backups.

Complete, differential and incremental backups

During recovery, the restore sequence needs to be equal to the backup sequence. Start with the last complete backup. When done, apply the differential backup followed by the incremental backups, if any, and finally apply the log backup until you reach the required Recovery Point Objective (RPO).

4.3.2 Log Backup

A log backup saves data from the log area to log backup files. SAP HANA can do this automatically at regular intervals. During a log backup, only the actual data of the log segments is written from the log area to log backup files or to a third-party backup server.

A log segment is backed up in the following situations:

▶ The log segment is full.
▶ After the configured time threshold has been exceeded.
▶ The database is started.

Overwrite by default

After installation, SAP HANA runs in log mode overwrite!

Monitor your log backups!

During normal operation, with log mode normal, keep automatic log backup activated. If not, and you forget to make log backups, the log area grows until the file system is full. When that happens, the database freezes!

4.3.3 Configuration Files

SAP HANA uses configuration files for configuration settings such as memory configuration parameter "global allocation limit". These configuration files do not reside in the database and, as such, are not included in the database backup. The configuration settings are not essential to perform a database recovery. The configuration settings of SAP HANA can easily be reset after a database recovery using the SAP HANA studio.

In a highly tuned SAP HANA system, you may want to back up the configuration files that contain the customer-specific configuration settings. Having these at hand somewhere safe will avoid you having to do a lot of re-configuring after the SAP HANA restore. If you want to back them up, you should do so manually.

Configuration files for HANA are written by default to specific directories (see Table 4.2).

Configuration settings	Location
Global configuration settings	`$DIR_INSTANCE/../SYS/global/hdb/custom/config`
Database specific configuration settings	`$DIR_INSTANCE/../SYS/global/hdb/custom/config/<database_name>`
Host specific configuration settings	`$SAP_RETRIEVAL_PATH`

Table 4.2: Configuration files of SAP HANA

Customer-specific SAP HANA settings

 Configuration files are only created in the above directories. If no customer-specific changes have been made, these directories are empty.

4.4   Backup Options

The following options exist to safeguard an SAP HANA database: backup to file system, backup using third party tools or backup using integrated storage solutions.

4.4.1   Backup to File System

Backup to file is straightforward and is possibly the oldest backup method for many database systems. It can be done from within the SAP HANA Studio, the Command Line Tool or even the DBA Cockpit. When you start file-based backup, the default backup destination is offered. But this can be overruled by specifying a different destination. Backups can be written to different locations, but all the parts of one particular data backup are written to the same destination.

In a distributed SAP HANA environment, SAP HANA automatically handles the synchronization of backups for all nodes. No special user intervention is needed. In the case of a backup to file, all nodes will write their backup to a shared backup file system (see Figure 4.2).

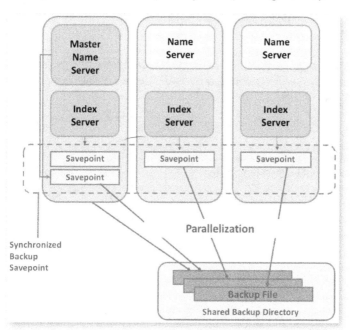

Figure 4.2: File backup in a distributed SAP HANA environment

4.4.2 Backup using Third Party Tools

In addition to backing up the SAP HANA database to the file system, you can back up and recover an SAP HANA database using a third-party tool that supports the Backint for SAP HANA. Backint is an API that enables 3rd party tool vendors to directly connect the backup agents to the SAP HANA database. Backint enables you to perform backup and recovery operations from SAP HANA studio and SAP HANA cockpit, using SQL commands, and even from the third party tool's graphical user interface.

One can assume that SAP HANA is not the only database in your system landscape. There are probably many other applications and databases which need to be backed-up on a regular basis. The advantage of Backint is that you can integrate the backup of SAP HANA into the backup schedule of a system landscape, SAP and non-SAP.

The third-party backup tool communicates with the SAP HANA database through the Backint for SAP HANA interface. Backint for SAP HANA uses named pipes to back up the content of the database.

In a distributed SAP HANA, each active host may have one or more volumes to be backed up. When Backint for SAP HANA is used to back up a database, several Backint communication processes are started, one for each volume.

Backup tools that use Backint for SAP HANA can only be installed on SAP HANA if they have been certified by SAP. Table 4.3 lists the certified backup tools.

Vendor	Backup Tool	On x86	On Power
Allen Systems	ASG-Time Navigator	Yes	No
CommVault	Simpana	Yes	No
CommVault	CommVault	No	Yes
CommVault	Hitachi Data Protection Suite	Yes	Yes
EMC	Networker, Interface for Data Domain Boost	Yes	No
HP	Data Protector, HP StoreOnce Plug-in for SAP HANA	Yes	No

Vendor	Backup Tool	On x86	On Power
IBM	Tivoli Storage Manager for Enterprise	Yes	No
IBM	Spectrum Protect for Enterprise Resource Planning	Yes	Yes
Libelle	BusinessShadow	Yes	No
Mindtree	NBU Connector for SAP HANA	No	Yes
SEP	SEP Sesam	Yes	Yes
Veritas Symantec	Net Backup	Yes	No

Table 4.3: Supported third-party backup tools

You can find more details on the certified tools in the Application Development Partner Directory; enter the search term "HANA-BRINT" and click on a partner name for further details[5].

4.4.3 Backup using Storage Snapshots

Storage snapshots are taken at storage level and are a backup or copy of all disks in a storage group at the same point in time.

Storage snapshots have the following benefits:

▶ They can be created with minimal impact on the system. This is because storage snapshots are created in the storage system and do not consume database services.

▶ Recovery from a storage snapshot is faster than recovery from a data backup.

▶ An SAP HANA database can be recovered to a specified point in time using a storage snapshot only or using storage snapshot in combination with log backups. This enables you to recover to a specified point in time.

---

[5] For more information on supported third party tools see
http://scn.sap.com/docs/DOC-62799

Storage snapshots and SAP HANA MDC

 Backup and recovery using snapshots is not yet available for Multi Database Containers (MDC).

There are two types of snapshots: database aware and database unaware snapshots.

Database Unaware Snapshots

A database unaware snapshot is a storage snapshot taken without notifying the database. When a recovery to the snapshot is done and the database restarted, the database assumes that a power-failure occurred and performs an online recovery. Database unaware snapshots are, by definition, inconsistent because the snapshot was taken while the database was running.

Database Aware Snapshots

A database aware snapshot is a storage snapshot which, when taken, notifies the database. As the database is warned, it can save a consistent state to disk. Database aware snapshots are, therefore, preferred over database unaware snapshots.

From an SAP HANA perspective, the storage snapshot captures the content of the SAP HANA data area at a particular point in time. Only use database aware snapshots. A snapshot is created by first creating an internal database snapshot. The database snapshot provides a view of the database with a consistent state at the point in time when it was created. The database snapshot is used to ensure the consistent state of the storage snapshot, regardless of the physical layout of the data area with respect to the number of disks, controllers, etc.

The following steps are needed to create a Storage Snapshot (see Figure 4.3):

1. Use the SAP HANA Studio or the Command Line Tool to initiate the database snapshot.

2. Use storage tools to create a storage snapshot.
3. Use the SAP HANA Studio or the Command Line Tool to confirm that the storage snapshot was created successfully. An ID is written to the backup catalog and the snapshot is released.

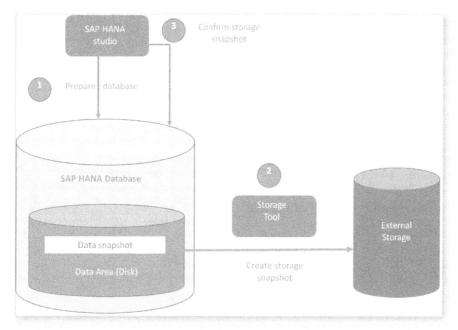

Figure 4.3: Steps for database aware snapshots

Integration between SAP HANA and Storage

 Database snapshots can be created via the SAP HANA Studio or the SQL command line. Both options are easy to use. For daily backups, the creation of the database snapshot will have to be automated by developing two scripts; one script to initiate the database snapshot and another to release the same snapshot. Both scripts will then have to be called from within the storage solution. Fortunately, most storage vendors provide such scripts by default.

4.4.4 Backup Options Comparative Table

Table 4.4 is an overview of the comparative features of a backup to a file system, a backup using third party tools or a backup using storage snapshots.

	File Backup	Third Party Tools	Storage Snapshot
Advantages	Integrity check at block level	Integrity check at block level Integrated into existing backup infrastructure Compression and encryption by backup tool Backup immediately available (no restore to file system needed)	Fast No network load Can be encrypted
Disadvantages	Requires additional storage Generates additional network load File system needs to be monitored (fill level) More time is needed to make backups available for recovery No compression	Generates additional network load	No integrity check at block level
Backup Size	Data only	Data only	Database size
Backup Duration	I/O based Network load Depends on the data size	I/O based Network load Depends on the data size	Negligible Seconds up to several minutes

Table 4.4: Comparison—Backup solutions

File backup seems to be the starting point for many customers. It is out-of-the-box and is easy to configure and administer. However, it has its limits. It is inconvenient for large SAP HANA databases and it is not integrated into the backup solutions used for other SAP and non-SAP applications and databases. In more mature or larger SAP HANA installations, a combination of third party tools and storage snapshots is appropriate.

5 Replication

Data Replication is an important part of business continuity and disaster recovery. For SAP HANA, two options are available: storage replication and system replication. Whether to use one or the other needs to be considered at an early stage of the implementation project, because they have an important impact on the future environment. Both options are discussed in this chapter.

Backups are scheduled daily, weekly and monthly. A drawback of this strategy is that there is a potential loss of data between the time of the last backup and the time of the failure. To improve data protection, the log buffer could be saved, for example, every 5 minutes, using automatic log backups. A database recovery in this strategy consists of the restore of the last backup followed by the application of log data.

There are two disadvantages in this procedure; first, the database can only be recovered up to the last available log backup, and second, applying log backups, especially when many exist, takes time as every entry in the log needs to be re-applied.

Therefore, a preferred solution is to provide continuous replication of all persisted data. This can be done via storage replication or system replication.

5.1 Storage Replication

The most basic replication method is disk, or RAID-1[6], mirroring for locally connected disks. Storage replication is an extension to local disk mirroring in which mirroring is extended across a storage network so that they can be located in distant locations in a master-slave model. The purpose of replication is to avoid damage from failures or disasters that may occur in the primary data center or, in case such events do occur, to improve the ability to recover by enabling or failing over to the secondary data center. For replication, latency is the key factor because it deter-

---

[6] RAID 1 consists of an exact copy of a set of data on two disks.

mines either how far apart the sites can be or the type of replication that can be employed. Figure 5.1 shows an example of storage replication.

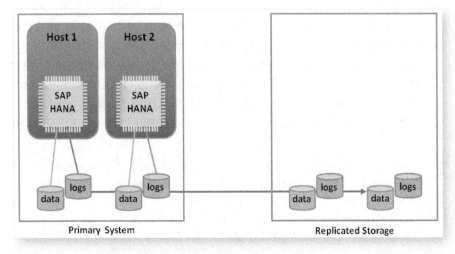

Figure 5.1: Storage replication

The main characteristic of such cross-site replication is how write operations are handled:

▶ Synchronous replication—guarantees "zero data loss" by means of atomic write operation. The write either completes on both sides or not at all. The write is not considered complete until acknowledged by both local and remote storage. Applications wait for the write transaction to complete before proceeding with further work. Inherently, performance drops proportionally depending on the distance between the local and remote storage.
An often-overlooked aspect of synchronous replication is the fact that failure of remote replica, or even just the interconnection, stops, by definition, any and all writes (freezing the local storage system). This is the behavior that guarantees zero data loss. However, many storage systems do not freeze but rather just proceed with local writes, losing the desired zero Recovery Point Objective (RPO) on the secondary storage system.

▶ The main difference between synchronous and asynchronous volume replication is that synchronous replication needs to wait for the destination storage whereas asynchronous replication does not. An asynchronous replication write is considered complete as soon as local storage acknowledges it. Remote storage is updated, but probably with a small time lag. Performance is greatly increased, but, in case a local storage is lost, the remote storage is not guaranteed to have the current copy of data and the most recent data may be lost.

▶ Semi-synchronous replication—a compromise between synchronous and asynchronous volume replication. Semi-synchronous means that a write is considered complete as soon as local storage acknowledges it and the remote storage acknowledges that it has received the write into cache memory. The actual remote write is not performed immediately but is performed asynchronously, resulting in better performance than synchronous replication and offering a better guarantee of durability than asynchronous replication.

▶ Point-in-time replication—introduces periodic snapshots that are replicated, instead of continuous replication. If the replicated snapshots are pointer-based, then during replication only the changed data is moved, not the entire volume.

Storage replication is done at hardware level. Apart from the initial setup, there is no effort in maintaining it, except when it all goes wrong. Data on the replication site cannot be accessed unless a disaster is declared and a failover is initiated. Every storage vendor has their own method to activate the secondary site. This, unfortunately, only enables access to the data in storage. The next step would be starting the hosts, databases and applications. This restart should not be underestimated, especially in environments with many SAP components such as SAP ERP, SAP BW and SAP CRM.

There are two start sequences which need to be respected when restarting the SAP components on the secondary site: an internal and an external sequence.

The internal start sequence refers to the SAP system itself. Every SAP system consists of several components. There are the ASCS instance, the application servers and the database system. When starting the SAP system, the database needs to start first, followed by the ASCS instance and then the application servers.

The external start sequence refers to all SAP components in the landscape. The SAP ERP system is, in most cases, the back-end system from which the satellite systems get their data. As such, it needs to start first, followed by SAP CRM, SAP SRM and the other systems.

VMware Site Recovery Manager

There are several disaster recovery management and automatization tools which, in combination with virtualization, are capable of enabling the storage on the secondary site and restarting all components in a predefined order. Some of these tools are also capable of simulating a disaster recovery procedure (DRP) in an isolated environment. VMware Site Recovery Manager is one of them.

Storage replication is invisible

Storage replication is done at storage level and is transparent to the database. The database system is totally unaware that this is happening. The storage system replicates groups of disks. It is unaware of what it is replicating. This implies that the configuration of such a solution should not be taken lightly. A top-down analysis is needed: from the SAP HANA database layout, to the file systems on the operating system, to the volume groups on the storage system.

5.2 System Replication

Database replication is called system replication in SAP HANA. It can be used on many database management systems, usually in a master and slave relationship between the primary and secondary database. The master database logs the changes to the data and sends them to the secondary, slave databases. The slave outputs a message stating that it has received the update successfully, thus allowing the sending of subsequent updates. Depending on high availability requirements and network latency, database replication can be done synchronously or asynchronously, or something in between. The difference between these options is when the primary database considers the change to be saved to the secondary system.

Database replication, or system replication as it is called in an SAP HANA context, is done between two or more SAP HANA instances. Usually system replication is set up so that a secondary standby system is configured as an exact copy of the active primary system with the same number of active hosts in each system. The number of standby hosts does not need to be identical. You can use a system with less CPU and memory if required (see Figure 5.2).

With multitier replication you replicate to more than one secondary system. One secondary system can be located near the primary system to serve as a rapid fail-over solution for planned downtime or to handle storage corruption or other local faults, while a second can be installed in a remote site to be used in a disaster recovery scenario.

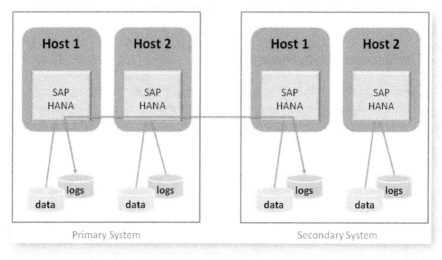

Figure 5.2: System replication

When the secondary system is started in recovery mode, it requests a snapshot of the data in the primary system. From then on, all logged changes in the primary system are replicated. Whenever logs are saved in the primary system, they are also sent to the secondary system.

5.2.1   Replication Modes

The following replication modes can be configured:

Synchronous in-memory

Synchronous in-memory is the default option. The primary system commits the transaction after it receives confirmation that the log has been received by the secondary system. In this option, the transaction is on the primary and written in memory on the secondary. This option provides best performance because it is not necessary to wait for disk I/O on the secondary system. Data will be lost if both systems fail at the same time. You can protect yourself from such a scenario by installing both systems in different data centers.

Synchronous with full sync option

Synchronous with full sync option means that log write is successful when the log buffer has been written to the log file of the primary and the secondary system. This is the most secure option but requires both systems to be of the same capacity. Slow I/O on the secondary will impact response time on the primary.

In addition, when the secondary system is disconnected because of network failure, the primary system suspends transaction processing until the connection to the secondary system is re-established. No data loss can occur in this scenario. Network latency needs to be verified because any hiccup will cause the primary to suspend all activity resulting in a performance impact for the applications and end-users.

Synchronous

With synchronous replication, the primary system does not commit a transaction until it receives confirmation that the log has been saved in the secondary system. Synchronous is comparable to Synchronous with full sync options, with one exception—if the connection to the secondary is lost, Synchronous synchronization will not suspend transaction processing interminably. It will wait until the synchronization time-out has been exceeded and then continue as if it was a standalone system.

This option guarantees no loss of data between both systems. However, the transaction is delayed by the same amount of time it takes to transmit the data to and persist it in the secondary system. As such, it is vulnerable to I/O performance and network latency.

Asynchronous

In asynchronous replication, the primary system sends redo log buffers to the secondary system asynchronously. The primary system sends the transaction to the secondary system through the network and commits the transaction to the log file of the primary. It does not wait for confirmation from the secondary system.

This option provides best performance because it is not necessary to wait for the secondary system. It is more vulnerable to data loss. Data changes may be lost on takeover. Asynchronous is a good option if there is a large distance between the primary and secondary system. It is a good option in multitier environments in which a secondary system is connected to the primary in synchronous mode and a third system in a remote site in asynchronous mode.

5.2.2   System Replication Comparative Table

The difference between the replication modes is the point in time in which they consider a transaction to be committed. This goes from the transaction needing to be saved to disk on both the primary and secondary up to it needing to be saved to disk on the primary and send to the secondary, not waiting for confirmation that the secondary received the transaction.

The second, and even more important, difference is what the primary does if the secondary is not reachable or is too slow.

Table 5.1 compares the SAP HANA replication modes in terms of when they consider data to be committed; what they do when the secondary is unavailable, and which technical aspects you should consider.

Mode	Details	Secondary unreachable	Considerations
Synchronous	Primary waits until secondary has received data and saved it to disk	Primary waits until log shipping timeout parameter is exceeded and continues without replication	Network latency Slow I/O on secondary system
Synchronous in memory	Primary system waits until secondary system has received data	Primary waits until log shipping timeout parameter is exceeded and continues without replication	Network latency
Synchronous full sync	Primary waits until secondary has received data and saved it to disk	Primary system is blocked until secondary system becomes available	Network latency Slow I/O on secondary system
Asynchronous	Primary system doesn't have to wait for secondary system	Primary system proceeds without replicating data	N/A

Table 5.1: Comparison—system replication configuration options

Synchronous full sync should be implemented at installations with very strict Recovery Point and Recovery Time Objectives. Dedicated SAP HANA appliances will have to be used and network latency needs to be considered because the primary will always wait for the secondary before confirming the data change to the application. The slightest drop in performance on the secondary system or network latency will have an impact.

Replication mode "synchronous in memory" is a valid alternative when the secondary system is installed on an appliance together with a non-production SAP-HANA system such as development or quality assurance. Note, that in the event of a failover, the non-production system will have to be halted.

Asynchronous replication is not acceptable for replication between two systems, because the primary does not even wait for confirmation from the secondary system. Asynchronous replication should only be considered in a multi replication scenario.

5.2.3 Features and Considerations

The following features should be considered when setting up or working with system replication:

► System replication cannot be set up using a backup and restore from the primary to the secondary. When replication is initially enabled, the secondary will request a data snapshot from the primary system.

► The secondary system does not immediately replay the received log. To avoid a growing list of logs, incremental data snapshots are transmitted asynchronously from the primary system to the secondary system. If the secondary system has to take over, only that part of the log that represents changes that were made after the most recent data snapshot needs to be replayed.

► In addition to logs and snapshots, the primary system also transfers information regarding which table columns are currently loaded into memory. The secondary system correspondingly preloads these columns. This improves performance in the event of failover because the secondary already has the same columns preloaded in memory.

► In the event of a system takeover, the secondary system becomes the primary system by replaying the last transaction logs, opening the database and then starting to accept queries.

Can you take backups on the secondary system?

 No you cannot, backups can only be taken on the primary system. If automatic log backup is enabled, the automatic log backup mechanism will be activated there after takeover.

> ## Can you use system replication for system copies?
>
> Yes, you can! Once the initial synchronization is complete, the secondary system can be activated or opened. It is much quicker than backup and restore. Tools exist to rename the database, if required. Be aware that in scale-out, the number of worker hosts needs to be the same as on the primary. The number of standby hosts can vary.

The secondary SAP HANA system is read-only and cannot be used for queries. It just sits there waiting to take over in case of a failure on the primary system. This is an expensive insurance policy since the SAP HANA server needs the same memory and CPU resources as the primary.

Fortunately, with SAP HANA system replication, you can host non-production SAP HANA systems on the secondary system under the following conditions:

- ▶ Table pre-load is turned off in the secondary system. This has a performance impact at takeover because used columns will not exist in the memory of the secondary system.
- ▶ The secondary system uses its own disk infrastructure. In the case of single node systems, this means extra storage is needed for the non-production SAP HANA systems.
- ▶ The non-production systems are stopped with the takeover of the production secondary.

Figure 5.3 shows an example system layout in which the secondary system is used for non-production SAP HANA systems.

When the primary system fails and a takeover is needed, the non-production systems will be stopped and the production system started. As table pre-load was not active on the secondary system, users will experience a temporary performance impact.

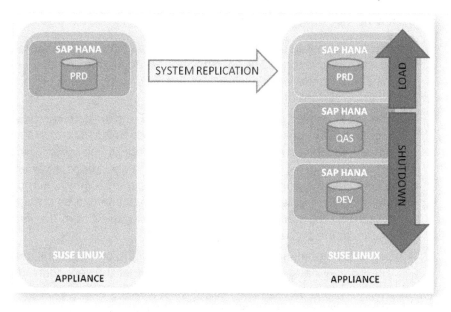

Figure 5.3: Secondary appliance hosting non-production systems

5.3 Log Shipping

Log shipping allows you to automatically send transaction log backups from a primary database to one or more secondary databases. The transaction log backups are applied to each of the secondary databases individually.

The difference between system replication (database replication) and log shipping is timing. In the first case, changes are immediately available on the secondary database. In the latter, a time difference between the primary and secondary can be configured so that logs are only applied on the secondary; for example, four hours after they were shipped from the primary to the secondary database.

Log shipping has the following characteristics:

▶ The log is sent to the secondary database as soon as it is backed up on the primary. This is configurable (for example, every 5 minutes). As the log is available on the secondary, data is protected from a failure of the primary site.

▶ The log is applied on the secondary database after a certain time. This is again configurable. This has the advantage that the secondary database is protected from any logical mistakes which might occur on the primary. If, for example, a user drops a key account, only the application of the logs needs to be interrupted on the secondary database. The secondary database can be brought online and the table containing the account copied from the secondary to the primary database.

▶ Log shipping has no performance impact on the primary database. The primary database does not have to wait for the secondary database. The shipping of the log is done independently from the database activities which might occur on the primary.

However, primary and secondary are not synchronized. This implies that when a disaster strikes, data can only be recovered up to the last log which was transferred to the target. Log shipping, therefore, has a potential impact on the Recovery Point Objective.

There is also an impact on the Recovery Time Objective because when a failover to the secondary is needed, the first step is the application of the not-yet applied logs to the secondary database, which might take some time.

Log shipping does not yet exist on SAP HANA

 Log shipping, as available in SQL Server or Oracle Standby Server, does not exist in SAP HANA. No doubt it will be in the future since the ability to intercept logical errors is a must-have for any database system. For the time being, you could configure regular database snapshots with storage snapshots to a remote data center in combination with automatic log backups, copied to a network file system on the secondary site. This method enables you to quickly start the SAP HANA database on the secondary site and apply the necessary logs from just before the logical mistake was made and, thus, intercept the error.

> ## Use storage solutions to simulate log shipping
>
> Storage solutions exist which provide continuous data protection with multiple recovery points. EMC Recover-Point, for example, is a storage-based solution which supports asynchronous and synchronous data replication of block-based storage. RecoverPoint uses block-based journaling comparable to transaction logging as known in traditional database systems. The journal allows rolling data to a previous "point-in-time" in order to view the storage content as it was before the data corruption.

5.4 Storage Replication versus System Replication versus Log Shipping

Although storage replication and system replication basically deliver the same result, there are some good reasons to implement one or the other. As Log shipping shares some similarities with replication, it can also be considered in the comparison (see Table 5.2).

	Storage Replication	System Replication	Log Shipping
Integrated Storage Solution (SAN)	Required	Not required	Not required
Replication	Inside Storage	Database tools	Scripting
Configuration	Inside Storage	Database tools	Scripting
Impact on performance	No	Limited	No
Impact on administration	Initial setup	Administration and monitoring needed	Administration and monitoring needed
Changes to the database (for example upgrade)	No impact	Reconfiguration needed	Reconfiguration needed

	Storage Replication	System Replication	Log Shipping
Protection against hardware failures	Yes	Yes	Yes
Protection against logical failures	No (unless via RecoverPoint)	No	Yes

Table 5.2: Comparison—storage replication, system replication and log shipping

Storage replication should always be the preferred option. Nothing needs to be configured, administered or maintained in the database. Storage replication is fully transparent, has no impact on performance and does not need to be taken into account when doing changes to the database instance. Needless to say that storage replication requires integrated storage, which is only available in the SAP HANA Tailored Datacenter (TDI) Integration option.

For customers using appliances, system replication is a very good alternative. It is out-of-the box, easy to use and offers more or less the same possibilities as storage replication does.

Log shipping should be considered if protection against logical errors is a requirement. With storage replication and system replication, everything which happens on the source is immediately applied to the target. With log shipping, a time difference between sending to the target database and applying to the target database can be configured. This time-gap allows for the interception of any logical errors on the target by interrupting replication.

To conclude, Table 5.3 compares the SAP HANA replication modes against storage replication. To be complete, we also included the backup recovery option in the comparison.

	SAP HANA Sync in memory	SAP HANA Sync	SAP HANA Asynch	Storage Replication	Backup & recovery
Replicate the entire system	DB only	DB only	DB only	Entire system	DB only
RTO	DNS switch	DNS switch and data load	DNS switch and data load	Start-up + data load	Recovery performance & amount of data to recover + start-up + data load
RPO	0	0	> 0	0	Last saved log
Performance impact	Network latency	Network latency	No	No	No
Supported for scale-up	Yes	Yes	Yes	Yes	Yes
Supported for scale-out	Yes	Yes	Yes	Yes	Yes

Table 5.3: Comparative table—replication options

The comparison shows that, depending on technical setup, a minimal RTO and RPO can be achieved with both SAP HANA system replication and storage replication. This is not the case with backup/recovery as it is limited to the speed of recovery and the availability of the last saved log.

6 High Availability

High availability means that a secondary system can immediately take over in case of a problem with the primary system, with little down time and no loss of data. This is an automated process in most cases. Clustering software and shared storage are required to do this. In this chapter, we discuss high availability and what it means in an SAP HANA context.

SAP HANA appliances are built for high availability. This is achieved due to redundancy—redundancy in the hardware, software, network and data center design.

SAP HANA provides several levels of defense against outages:

▶ Hardware Redundancy—The SAP HANA appliance has multiple layers of redundant hardware and network components such as redundant power supplies and fans, error-correcting memories, redundant network switches and uninterrupted power supply (UPS). The disk storage system uses striping to provide redundancy from disk failures. These redundancy solutions are in the design of the appliance and are fully transparent to the operating system and SAP HANA database.

▶ Software Redundancy—SAP HANA is installed on SUSE Linux Enterprise or Red Hat Enterprise Linux for SAP. The operating system is pre-configured and only contains the operating system features used by SAP HANA. Additionally, the SAP HANA software also includes a watchdog function which automatically re-starts the SAP HANA services when needed.

▶ Data Persistence—SAP HANA is an in-memory database but persists data to disks to support system restart and recovery from host failures, with minimal delay and without loss of data.

▶ High Availability - A standby host can be used for failover in case of failure of the primary hosts.

6.1 High Availability versus Disaster Recovery?

High availability should not be confused with disaster recovery. High availability means that a secondary system can immediately take over in case of a problem with the primary system, with little down time and no loss of data. This is an automated process in most cases. Clustering software and shared storage are required to do this. As data is shared between the nodes of the cluster, the clustering software can easily handle failover and failback.

The difference between high availability and disaster recovery is that the former is used to protect the application and database from a hardware failure, whereas the latter is used to protect against a disaster at datacenter level. High availability restarts the application as fast as possible on the secondary node, whereas disaster recovery recovers and restarts all applications in a secondary data center. For disaster recovery, things like Recovery Point Objective (RPO) and Recovery Time Objective (RTO) come into play.

6.2 High Availability Clusters

A high availability cluster consists of several computers or nodes which cooperate to support databases and applications. High availability clusters use cluster software to operate and monitor the nodes of the cluster and the different applications and databases running on those cluster nodes. Should one of the applications, databases or nodes fail, the cluster software will attempt to restart the impacted application or database on one of the remaining nodes of the cluster. This is known as failover. The failover operation consists of several steps: mounting of the file systems, reconfiguring the network, opening the databases and finally, starting the applications. As soon as the failed node is rebuilt or restored, the application or database can be failed-back to the original node. Without clustering, if a server running a particular application crashes, the application will be unavailable until the crashed server is fixed.

A high availability cluster is not only about the clustering software. Every component in the design needs to be considered as a single point of failure and redundancy needs to be built in, including multiple network connections and data storage which is redundantly connected via storage area networks. Clustering software usually uses a heartbeat network connection to monitor the health and status of each node in the cluster.

The software must also be able to handle a split-brain situation which occurs when all of the network connections go down simultaneously but the cluster nodes are still running. If that happens, each node in the cluster may mistakenly decide that every other node has gone down and attempt to start applications and databases that other nodes are still running. This may cause data corruption on the shared storage.

As applications and databases may run on different nodes at any point in time, a logical hostname must be used. The logical host is a network address assigned to the application or databases protected by the cluster (see Figure 6.1). This logical hostname identity is not tied to a single cluster node. It is actually a virtual network address/hostname that is linked with the application or database protected by the cluster. If, for example, a cluster node with a running database goes down, the database will be restarted on another cluster node and the network address that is used to access the application will be brought up on the new node as well so that users can access the application again.

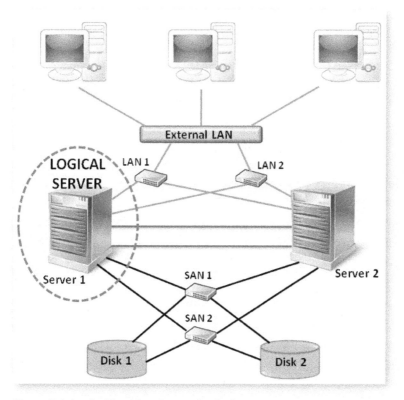

Figure 6.1: Logical host in a two-node cluster

These features help minimize the chances that the clustering failover will be required. At failover, the impacted application or database is unavailable until it is restarted on one of the remaining nodes. This can take some time, especially if the database needs to do an online recovery.

Depending on the clustering software, clusters can consist of several nodes. With Microsoft Windows Server 2012, for example, failover clustering can support to up 64-nodes in a single cluster.

The most common size for an HA cluster is a two-node cluster since that is the minimum required to provide redundancy.

In SAP environments, high-availability clusters are most commonly configured as follows:

▶ Active & active—The load is divided among all nodes in the cluster. An SAP application server is installed on every node. Nowadays, this concept is standard in SAP environments.

▶ Active & passive—One node is actively used while the other is used as a backup node. This used to be the way of using cluster software in combination with SAP. You might still come across these types of installations on older UNIX releases. In this setup, a non-production system is installed on the secondary node. This system is halted at failover of the production system.

6.2.1 Application Requirements

In order to run in a high-availability cluster environment, an application must satisfy the following minimum technical requirements:

▶ There must be an easy way to start, stop, force-stop, and check the status of the application. This means the application must have a command line interface or scripts to control the application including support for multiple instances of the application. This is the case for SAP applications. From an operating system perspective, SAP consists of a number of processes which can easily be started, stopped and killed using a command line interface which is similar on all operating systems.

▶ The application must be able to use shared storage. This is the case for SAP and all databases supported by SAP.

► Data consistency must be guaranteed by the application. All SAP data is stored inside the database. The database system is, therefore, responsible for data consistency. Databases do an online recovery when they are restarted after an unexpected shutdown. As such, data consistency is guaranteed.

6.2.2 SAP Components

The first step in the implementation of high availability is the identification of the single points of failure (SPOFs) from an SAP NetWeaver Application Server perspective.

An SAP system consists of the following components:

The database system

All customization and business data resides in the database. As such, the database is the most important component in the SAP system landscape. Many SAP system administrators and consultants do not realize that SAP Application Servers consist of the SAP kernel and several configuration files. The SAP kernel can be compared to an interpreter. It reads ABAP code from within the database and executes it on the platform it runs. If one of my customers called me today saying that all is lost except for the last database backup, I would tell them not to worry—we will be able to recover.

SAP Central Services

The SAP Central Services Instance consists of Message and Enqueue Services.

For ABAP-based systems, it is called ABAP SAP Central Services (ASCS). For Java-based systems it is just called SAP Central Services (SCS). The SAP Central Services consists of the SAP Message and Enqueue Services.

SAP Message Service

The Message Service is used to exchange and regulate messages between SAP Instances or Application Servers. It is responsible for the load balancing of the users during client connects.

SAP Enqueue Service

The Enqueue Service manages the locking of business objects at the SAP transaction level. Locks are set in a lock table stored in the shared memory of the host on which the Enqueue Service runs. Failure of this service has a considerable effect on the system because all transactions that contain locks must be rolled back and any SAP updates being processed fail.

Primary Application Server

Nowadays, the Primary Application Server (PAS) is an application server like any other. In older SAP releases, this was called the Central Instance and included the Central Services, Message and Enqueue Service. The only difference between the Primary Application Server and the other application servers is that the PAS is still the location where an SAP upgrade is to be done.

Additional Application Servers

Depending on the size of the SAP system, transaction load or number of concurrent users, the Primary Application Server might not be enough. As such, additional application servers may be installed.

Replicated Enqueue Server

The Replicated Enqueue Server runs on another host and contains a replica of the lock table. If the ASCS instance with the Enqueue Service fails, it must be restarted on the host on which the replication server is running. The restarted Enqueue Service will copy the lock table from the Replicated Enqueue Server to generate the new lock table.

To summarize, an SAP system consists of the following mandatory components of which the database and ASCS instance are single points of failure (see Table 6.1):

Component	Number of components in an SAP system	Single Point of Failure
ASCS instance (message and Enqueue server)	1	YES
Database instance	1	YES
Primary application server (PAS)	1	No (if you install at least 1 additional application server)
Additional application servers	X	No (if you install more than 1)
Enqueue Replication Server	At least 2	No

Table 6.1: Mandatory SAP components and SPOFs

Figure 6.2 shows a high-availability cluster configuration where the SAP Single Point of Failure (SPOF), the ASCS instance and the database are installed in the cluster while the non-SPOF components (the primary application server (PAS), additional application server and Enqueue replication servers) are installed locally on the cluster nodes. Additional application server instances are installed outside the cluster on separate hosts.

If a hardware or software problem occurs on the first cluster node, the clustered ASCS instance and/or database automatically fail over to another node. If you need to maintain the cluster node when the ASCS instance and/or database are running, you can switch the instance to another node. When maintenance work is finished, you move them back to the original node.

The ASCS, which contains the Enqueue or lock table, is in memory. When the ASCS instance is restored or failed-over, all content of the Enqueue table is gone. This results in ABAP dumps for all applications doing an update at the time of the fail-over. Installed Enqueue replication servers on both nodes can protect the in-memory Enqueue table. Every entry in the Enqueue table is replicated to the replication servers. At restart or failover, the ASCS instance will copy the in-memory Enqueue table from the replication server. As such, no Enqueue or locks get lost.

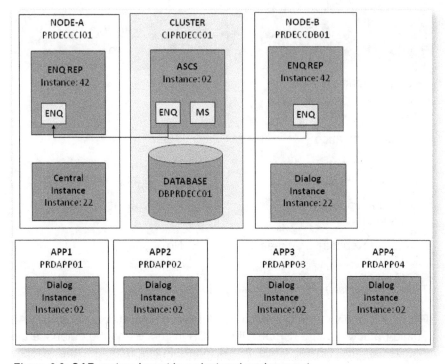

Figure 6.2: SAP system layout in a clustered environment

To protect system components that are non-SPOFs, for example, application servers, you have to install more than one.

Consider the following options:

▶ Install the primary application server and the additional application server instance on the cluster nodes of a cluster. The advantage of this layout is that both nodes are constantly in use (active-active layout). Any additional application server instances are installed on hosts outside the cluster.

▶ Install the primary application server and all additional application server instances on hosts which are not part of a cluster.

6.2.3   High Availability Clusters and SAP HANA

SAP is an in-memory database and, as such, a restart is expensive. During the startup, the persistency files are opened; the Row Store tables are loaded into memory; transactions committed but not yet written to the data area are rolled forward; open transactions are rolled back; and finally, a save point is taken. The database is available after performing the save point. However, the startup is not yet finished because the Column tables still have to be loaded. This is fortunately done asynchronously. Therefore, restarting a large SAP HANA database should be avoided at all cost. Protecting the SAP HANA database using cluster software is, therefore, not the best option. A failover always results in a restart of the SAP HANA database.

SAP installations with low Recovery Point and Recovery Time Objectives should consider SAP HANA system replication using a secondary SAP HANA system with data preloaded in memory.

With system replication, you can replicate your SAP HANA database data from one system to another system to compensate for failures. By default, when the primary system fails, the secondary system waits for further instructions. There is no automatic failover mechanism. The administrator has to manually initiate the takeover. This might be problematic at 1 a.m. in the morning when nobody is in the office.

Automated high availability for single node systems can be achieved by combining system replication with high availability cluster software such as SUSE Linux Enterprise High Availability and the Red Hat Enterprise Linux High Availability Add-on for SAP HANA.

The add-on uses the SAP HANA resource agent to check the SAP system replication. When installed and configured, the agent provides the automated takeover mechanism for SAP HANA system replication (see Figure 6.3).

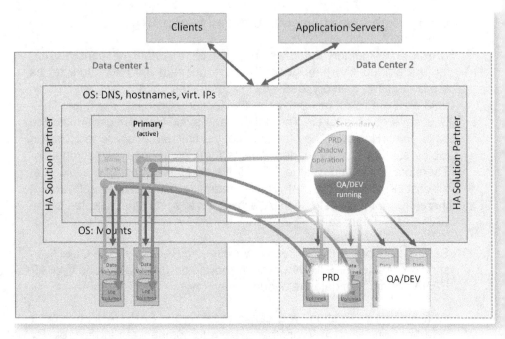

Figure 6.3: SAP HANA in a High Availability Cluster

SAP HANA system replication in combination with high availability software provides the following functionality:

▶ synchronous replication between the primary and secondary system

▶ automatic failover to the secondary system when the primary fails

▶ automatic shutdown of any non-production system, which may be running on the secondary system, before opening the secondary system for productive use

▶ switch the DNS alias from the primary to the secondary node to enable the SAP HANA clients to reconnect to the database

7 Virtualization

Virtualization refers to the creation of a virtual machine that looks like a real computer with hardware resources such as CPU, memory and storage, and an operating system. Software executed on these virtual machines is separated from the underlying hardware resources.

The host machine is the actual machine on which the virtualization takes place, and the guest machine is the virtual machine. The words 'host' and 'guest' are used to distinguish the software that runs on the physical machine from the software that runs on the virtual machine. The software or firmware that creates a virtual machine on the host hardware is called a hypervisor.

Advantages of virtualization:

Consolidation

Virtualization allows multiple servers to be consolidated onto one physical server, with little or no decrease in overall performance.

Ease of Provisioning

Virtualization encapsulates the server into an image that can be duplicated or moved, greatly reducing the cost of provisioning and deployment.

Manageability

Virtual machines can be moved from server to server with no downtime, which simplifies common operations like hardware maintenance and reduces planned downtime.

Availability

High Availability ensures that in the event of an unplanned hardware failure, affected virtual machines are restarted on another host.

Software virtualization is done by software, or a so-called hypervisor, which emulates a physical machine. The difference between software and hardware virtualization is that with software virtualization the same hardware platform is shared between the hypervisor and the virtual machine. Software virtualization on an x86 hardware platform will only be able to operate virtual machines capable of running on that platform. The hypervisor divides the hardware resources among the different virtual machines or guests. The biggest advantage of virtualization is that hardware resources can be better divided according to the needs of the different virtual systems. These guest operating systems are unaware of the fact that they are running on a virtualized environment. Examples of software virtualization are VMware and Microsoft Hyper-V.

7.1   Virtualization on VMware

VMware vSphere is a virtualization platform that creates a layer of abstraction between the resources required by an application and operating system, and the underlying hardware that provides those resources. SAP has been supported on VMware for a very long time. All SAP applications that are based on SAP NetWeaver 04 SR1 or SAP BASIS 6.40 SP09 and higher, and which are supported on Windows 64-bit in a non-virtualized environment, are also supported in a virtualized environment.

What is currently supported by SAP for SAP HANA?

► A single SAP HANA virtual machine on a dedicated SAP HANA certified server is supported.

► Multiple SAP HANA virtual machines on a single physical server and scale-out scenarios are now supported in general availability.

► The maximum size of a virtual SAP HANA instance is limited by the maximum size of a virtual machine. On VMware vSphere 5.5, this is 64 vCPUs and 1 TB of memory.

► Each SAP HANA instance / virtual machine must be sized according to the existing SAP HANA sizing guidelines and VMware recommendations.

► CPU and memory overcommitting must not be used. Please note that CPU and memory overcommitting are also not recommended for non-SAP HANA databases.

► VMware vMotion, VMware Distributed Resource Scheduled (DRS) and VMware HA are supported with SAP HANA.

Please note the following restrictions when deploying SAP HANA on VMware for the production systems:

▶ The virtual CPUs (vCPUs) of a single VM must be pinned to physical cores so that only one single VM exclusively uses the CPU cores of a socket.

▶ CPU and Memory overcommitting must not be used.

▶ The defined KPIs for Data Throughput and Latency for production SAP HANA systems has to be fulfilled for each VM. SAP has released a special tool, the SAP HANA HW Configuration Check Tool, to measure if the used storage is able to deliver the required IO capacity (see SAP Note 1943937 for more details).

7.1.1 High Availability

VMware High Availability (HA) clusters enable a collection of physical servers or ESX hosts to work together as a group and to provide higher levels of availability for virtual machines than each server host could provide individually (see Figure 7.1).

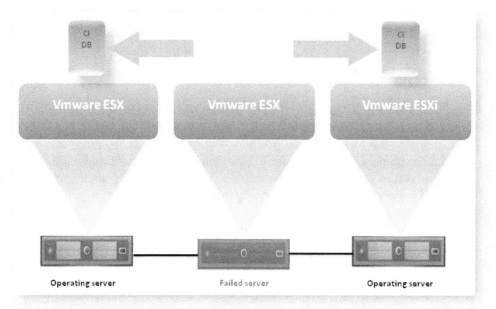

Figure 7.1: VMware vSphere High Availability

127

The physical servers or ESX hosts in the cluster are monitored and, in the event of a failure, the virtual machines on the failed host are restarted on different hosts.

Using VMware High Availability (HA) to protect an SAP HANA system is probably the easiest and most cost-efficient way to protect a virtualized SAP HANA system against OS and hardware failures. In the event of a failover, the entire VM is restarted. Because VMware HA is done at VM level, no specific storage tasks or cluster solutions are required. There is even no dependency on DNS as both hostname and IP fail-over.

It is important to note that VMware HA only protects the VM. If something goes wrong with the operating system or SAP HANA database, VMware HA will not detect anything.

However,

- ▶ SAP HANA comes with an auto-restart service watchdog which automatically detects and restarts stopped services.
- ▶ SAP HANA application or operating system failures can be detected with third party software solutions. These will attempt to restart SAP HANA several times. When unsuccessful, they will initiate a VM restart.

7.1.2 Fault Tolerance

With VMware Fault Tolerance (FT), a secondary virtual machine resides on a different ESX host and executes exactly the same sequence of instructions as the primary virtual machine. Put simply, Fault Tolerance is a kind of in-memory RAID-1 mirroring. Everything which is executed on the primary virtual machine is also executed on the secondary virtual machine. If the primary fails, the secondary is available instantly.

The secondary is ready to take over at any time without any data loss or interruption of service should the primary fail. Both virtual machines are managed as a single unit but run on different physical hosts (see Figure 7.2).

Because VMware Fault Tolerance is suitable for workloads with a maximum of four vCPUs and 64GB of memory, it can be used for SAP components such as the ASCS which is critical and a single point of failure (SPOF) but does not have a large resource requirement.

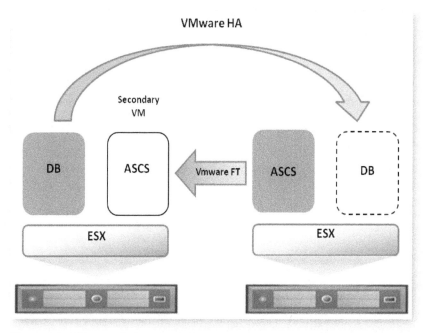

Figure 7.2: VMware vSphere Fault Tolerance

7.1.3 SAP System Layout

Using a combination of VMware High Availability and Fault Tolerance can increase high availability. Such an environment would consist of the following components (see Figure 7.3):

▶ An ABAP Central Services (ASCS) instance protected by Fault Tolerance. Currently VMware FT supports only four vCPUs and 64GB of memory. An ASCS instance does not need a lot CPU power and is, as such, a good candidate for VMware FT. An additional advantage of VMware FT is that the Enqueue Replication Server one would install in a standard high availability cluster is not needed here.

▶ A database instance protected by VMware High Availability. HA monitors the VMware ESX host in the cluster and detects hardware failures. VMware HA can be extended with Symantec ApplicationHA for the monitoring of the database. Symantec ApplicationHA will attempt to restart the database when it fails. It will trigger VMware HA to failover the host after several unsuccessful attempts.

> ► SAP systems with high performance requirements enforced by additional application servers running on separate virtual machines.

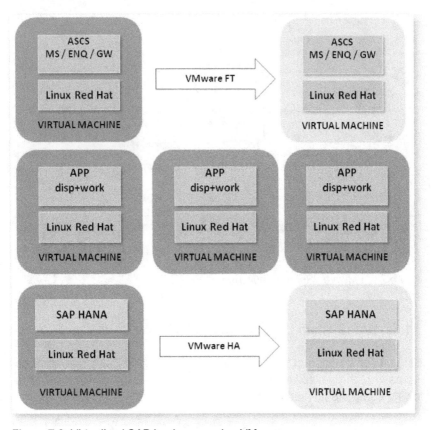

Figure 7.3: Virtualized SAP landscape using VMware

7.1.4 Monitoring Tools

VMware High Availability and Fault Tolerance monitor the Virtual Machine. If something goes wrong with the underlying physical hardware, VMware will restart (HA) or activate (FT) the VM on another ESX host. Unfortunately, VMware does not monitor the operating system, application or database. If something goes wrong with these, nothing happens, nothing is restarted. VMware has an API that enables third-party vendors to develop agents that can monitor the health of an application running within the guest OS and inform VMware when a problem is detected and trigger a restart.

The application agent runs a utility to verify the status of the application. If an application failure is detected, an attempt is made to restart the application. If unsuccessful after a number of attempts, a restart of the VM is triggered. Third-party tools such as Symantec ApplicationHA provide monitoring capabilities for applications running inside VMs.

7.1.5 Moving Virtual Machines

VMware vMotion enables the migration or movement of virtual machines from one physical host to another while the virtual machine is running. The move is done online without any service interruption. VMotion is also supported with SAP HANA.

In case an SAP HANA host experiences increased hardware alerts or if hardware maintenance is required, the system administrator can proactively migrate the SAP HANA databases that reside on the host to another physical host in order to avoid downtime or costs to the business.

SAP HANA runs in-memory and has a large memory footprint. As such, a restart takes time. When executing a live migration, while query or transaction processing continues, the entire state of the SAP HANA memory is copied from one physical host to another, with only a slight performance hit until the migration is completed.

Moving large VM's using VMotion

 SAP HANA is an in-memory database. Data changes, delta merges, and garbage collectors constantly modify the content of the memory areas. Using VMotion to move a large virtual machine from one ESX server to the next might take a very long time, because the memory areas are large and change quickly in order to be able to copy them in a reasonable amount of time. However, if system maintenance on the hardware layer is necessary and downtime is unacceptable; using VMotion is a valid alternative to move virtual machines.

7.2 Virtualization on IBM Power VM

SAP customers have been running their SAP applications on POWER for many years, using virtualization capabilities to re-configure or re-balance their environments.

As of November 2015, SAP HANA is also supported on IBM POWER 8. In May 2016, support was extended to S/4 HANA.

SAP supports virtualization on POWER with some restrictions to the division of CPU, memory and I/O resources. These limitations only apply to production SAP HANA systems. Non-production systems have far greater flexibility.

Consider the following restrictions which apply when running an SAP HANA production system on Power VM:

▶ Only POWER 8 is supported.
▶ Production SAP HANA systems must reside in either a dedicated or dedicated-donating virtual machine or logical partition (LPAR).
▶ Minimum LPAR size is 4 cores with 128 GB of memory.
▶ LPARs can be resized but the core-to-memory (CTM) ratio needs to be respected.
▶ Only SUSE Linux Enterprise for SAP is supported. Red Hat Enterprise Linux for SAP is not yet supported.

For non-production SAP HANA systems:

▶ POWER 7 systems can be used for non-production SAP HANA systems (test and development).
▶ The core-to-memory (CTM) ratio does not apply.
▶ Minimum LPAR size is 2 cores with 64GB of memory.

An advantage of IBM POWER is that traditional SAP and non-SAP applications using Linux, AIX or IBM i operating systems can be collocated on the same SAP HANA system. Figure 7.4 illustrates different LPARs residing on the same Power VM Hypervisor.

In this example, SAP HANA, SAP and non-SAP applications share the same infrastructure. The SAP HANA production LPARs are operated in dedicated-donating mode. In this mode, unused CPU cycles of the production SAP HANA LPARs are given to the shared processor pool. Unused CPU cycles can be used by the non-SAP HANA applications while immediate CPU access for the SAP HANA processes remains guaranteed.

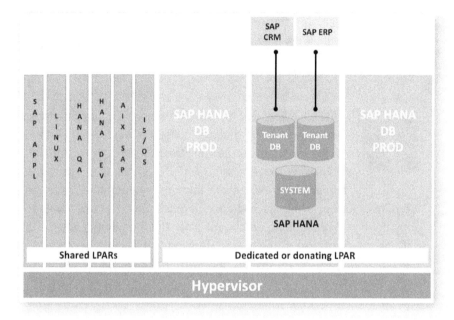

Figure 7.4: SAP HANA layout on Power VM

The SAP HANA multitenant database container functionality can be used to combine small SAP HANA databases which need far fewer resources than the minimum LPAR with 4 cores and 128 GB of memory.

Another advantage is that POWER VM allows you to resize LPARs as you go. SAP HANA, however, does not yet support this. This means that in order to re-size an LPAR, the database must be restarted.

7.2.1   Live Partition Mobility

POWER VM Live Partition Mobility provides the ability to move logical partitions from one system to the next. A live partition migration will duplicate the exact same environment of the current partition on the destination server. During the migration process, there is a very short period of time where processing is suspended on the source server before the partition is resumed on the destination server. To an end-user this might look like a temporary increase in response time. The running transaction will continue seamlessly after the switch.

POWER VM Live Partition Mobility is fully supported for SAP HANA workloads. It eliminates the need to stop an application in order to re-balance the system landscape, to react to changes in capacity needs, or to perform system maintenance or upgrades.

Using Live Partition Mobility on large SAP HANA systems

 SAP HANA is an in-memory database. Data changes, delta merges and garbage collectors modify the content of the memory areas constantly. Using Live Partition Mobility to move a large SAP HANA partition from one server to the next might take a very long time, because the memory areas are large and change quickly in order to be able to copy them in a reasonable amount of time. But if getting downtime is difficult, an alternative is to use Live Partition Mobility in order to move partitions between servers when hardware maintenance on the hardware layer is due.

8 Conclusion and Summary

In this chapter, we compare the different solutions discussed in this book. The chapter comes with decision flowcharts which you can use in your organization to choose the proper technology for your environment and specific needs.

During the architecture design and setup phase of the implementation project, decisions need to be made concerning high-availability and disaster recovery.

Throughout this book, we explained the technology options available to deploy SAP HANA, the principles for backup and recovery, data replication, high-availability and virtualization, the things to consider and the available technology to choose from in order to implement a well-considered scenario.

8.1 Cluster Software versus Virtualization

High Availability can be accomplished through cluster software or via virtualization. Both have their advantages and disadvantages.

8.1.1 Comparative Table

Table 8.1 lists the differences between the options of high availability with cluster software and the virtualization layer.

	VM Restart	Application Monitoring	Failover / Service Restart Time	Hardware Maintenance Downtime	OS Maintenance Downtime	Cost / Complexity
VMware HA	YES	NO	HIGH	NONE	HIGH	LOW
VMware HA + Fault Tolerance	YES	NO	NONE	NONE	HIGH	MED
VMware HA + Symantec Application HA	YES	YES	MED	NONE	HIGH	MED
Guest Failover Cluster	NO	YES	LOW	MED	LOW	HIGH
VMware HA + Guest Failover Cluster	YES	YES	LOW	NONE	LOW	HIGH

Table 8.1: High availability with clusters or virtualization

To summarize:

▶ Restart—The cluster software will only restart the application and database on the secondary node, whereas with virtualization, the virtual machine which contains the operating system, the database and the application is restarted on another physical server.

▶ Application monitoring—Cluster software will monitor the application and attempt to restart it several times on the current node before failing over to the secondary node. Virtualization, by default, only monitors the virtual machine. If the application fails, VMware will not react. This can be overcome by extending VMware with tools which monitor the application and, if needed, initiate a restart of the application, database or of the complete virtual machine.

▶ Hardware—Hardware maintenance has no impact on virtualized systems as they can be moved online to another physical host. Hardware maintenance on one of the cluster nodes results in at least one restart of all applications installed on the impacted node because they need to failover to the secondary node.

▶ Operating system maintenance cannot be intercepted with virtualization as the virtual machine includes the operating system. With cluster software it can because the applications running on the node to be patched can be moved to the secondary node.

▶ Operating system corruption cannot be intercepted with virtualization. VMware will restart the virtual machine on another physical server. If the operating system is corrupted, it remains corrupted. As such, an operating system recovery is needed. This is not the case with cluster software. The corrupted node can easily be recovered or re-installed while the applications run on the secondary node.

▶ Cost and complexity—High availability through virtualization is easy. In VMware vCenter, right+click on the VM and enable HA or FT, and then it is active. This is not the case with cluster software. Software clusters have many prerequisites and are complex, and the installation and configuration take time.

▶ Availability—Cluster software offers better protection than virtualization because the dependency between the operating system layer and the application or database is cut. This is not the case with virtualization. In virtualization, the operating system and application are seen as one.

Our recommendation: use cluster software to achieve the greatest high-availability for your production and critical systems. This can be extended with the virtualization layer to remove the dependency between the operating system and the hardware layer. Many SAP customers use VMware HA for less-critical systems such as development and acceptance systems, because it is so easy to implement and use.

SAP HANA system replication and Clustering Software

 SAP HANA system replication is often combined with clustering software to protect against system failures. It enables monitoring of the SAP HANA instance with automatic failover and allows operating system and SAP HANA instance upgrades on one node, while the other node is running the SAP HANA database.

8.1.2 Decision Flow

High Availability can be accomplished through cluster software or via the virtualization layer. In Section 8.1.1, we discussed the advantages and disadvantages.

The flow shown in Figure 8.1 should guide you through the decision making process when deciding to go for a standard high-availability cluster or high-availability through virtualization. In this example, we compare the Symantec VERITAS Cluster with VMware virtualization. Please note that the flow is applicable to other cluster software and virtualization solutions as well.

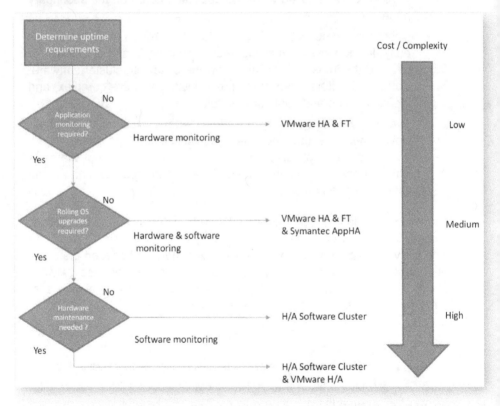

Figure 8.1: High availability versus virtualization decision flow

The purpose of the flow is to determine uptime requirements and a possible high-availability solution.

Question 1—Is application monitoring required?

Cluster software will monitor the application and attempt to restart it on the same node when it stops. When unsuccessful, a failover is initiated to the secondary node and an attempt is made to restart the application there.

VMware High Availability or Fault Tolerance monitors the virtual machine, not the application. If software monitoring is required, you should go to the second question. If not, high availability on the virtualization layer is sufficient for your setup.

Question 2—Rolling OS upgrades?

In a high-availability cluster, operating system patching and upgrades are possible with a minimum amount of downtime. The secondary node can be upgraded without downtime. When finished, the application is restarted on the secondary node and the primary can be completed. As such, downtime is limited to a restart of the application. The high-availability cluster also protects against any operating system corruption because the application is virtualized from the operating system.

VMware High Availability or Fault Tolerance restarts the virtual machine. This includes the operating system, database and application. Therefore, an operating system upgrade without downtime is not feasible. In addition, as the VM includes the operating system, there is no protection against operating system corruptions.

If rolling upgrades or protection from operating system corruptions are not necessary, you can proceed with virtualization. If you answered 'yes' to the first question (application monitoring is required), you can extend VMware with application monitoring through, for example, Symantic AppHA. As with the cluster software, AppHA will attempt to restart the application several times. If this fails, it will trigger VMware to restart the whole virtual machine.

If you also answered 'yes' to the second question, you should implement a high-availability cluster. High availability through virtualization will not be sufficient for your setup.

Question 3—Should hardware maintenance be possible without downtime?

If the answer is 'yes', you should extend the High-Availability cluster with virtualization. The advantage of virtualization is that the dependency between the operating system and hardware is removed. This is not the case with high-availability software clusters because a hardware replacement results in a re-installation of the operating system on the replaced node and re-configuring of the cluster setup.

Finally, note the complexity bar! The more solutions you combine, the more complex it gets!

8.2 Storage Replication versus System Replication

SAP HANA databases can be replicated via storage replication or via built-in SAP HANA functionality system replication. Both have their advantages and disadvantages.

8.2.1 Storage Replication

One drawback of traditional backups is the potential loss of data between the time of the last backup and the time of the failure. A preferred solution, therefore, is to provide continuous replication of all data. Several SAP hardware partners offer a storage-level replication solution which delivers a backup of the volumes and file-systems to a remote, networked storage system.

8.2.2 System Replication

Usually, system replication is set up so that a secondary database is configured as an exact copy of the active primary database system. With multitier system replication, you have one primary SAP HANA system and can have multiple secondary systems. The secondary SAP HANA system can be located near the primary system to serve as a rapid failover solution for planned downtime or it can be installed in a remote site to be used in a disaster recovery.

8.2.3 Transaction Log Shipping

Log shipping allows you to automatically send transaction log backups from a primary database on a primary server instance to one or more secondary databases on separate secondary server instances. The transaction log backups are applied to each of the secondary databases individually.

The difference between system replication and log shipping is timing. In the first case, changes are immediately available on the secondary database. In the latter, a time difference between the primary and secondary can be configured so that logs are only applied on the secondary, for example, four hours after they were shipped from the primary to the secondary database.

8.2.4 Comparative Table

Although all three solutions basically deliver the same capabilities, there are some good reasons to implement one of these (see Table 8.2)

	Storage Replication	System Replication	Log Shipping
Integrated Storage Solution (SAN)	Required	Not required	Not required
Replication	Inside Storage	Database tools	Scripting[7]
Configuration	Inside Storage	Database tools	Scripting
Impact on performance	No	Limited	No
Impact on administration	Initial setup	Administration and monitoring needed	Administration and monitoring needed

---

[7] Log shipping, as available in SQL Server or Oracle Standby Server, does not exist in SAP HANA. It can be scripted by using a combination of database snapshots, storage replication and log backups.

	Storage Replication	System Replication	Log Shipping
Changes to the database (for example, upgrade)	No impact	Reconfiguration needed	Reconfiguration needed
Protection against hardware failures	Yes	Yes	Yes
Protection against logical failures	No (unless third party tools)	No	Yes

Table 8.2: Comparison—storage replication, system replication and log shipping

Data protection can be accomplished through storage replication, system replication and transaction log shipping. Every solution has advantages and disadvantages.

8.2.5 Decision Flow

The flow shown in Figure 8.2 should guide you through the decision making process when deciding to use storage replication, system replication or transaction log shipping.

Question 1—Do you need protection against logical data loss?

With storage replication and system replication both primary and secondary are always synchronized. Asynchronous synchronization is available to overcome network latency when there is a large distance between the primary and secondary sites. It is, however, not meant to intercept a logical or human error on the primary, because synchronization is a matter of seconds maybe minutes, before the change is applied on the secondary.

With transaction log shipping, a time difference between the primary and secondary can be configured so that logs are only applied on the secondary, for example, four hours after they were shipped from the primary to the secondary database. Transaction log shipping results in a longer

Recovery Time Objective because at failover, the secondary system needs to apply all remaining logs before it becomes available.

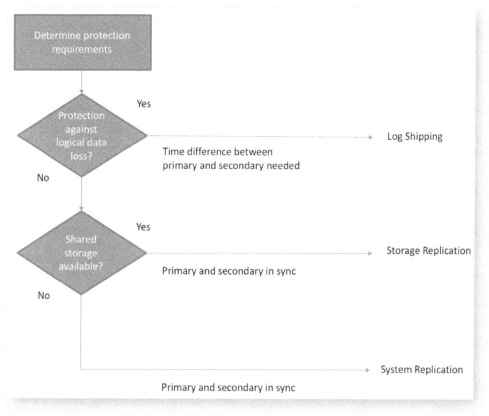

Figure 8.2: Decision flow—storage replication, system replication & log shipping

If you need protection against logical or human errors and a longer Recovery Time Objective is acceptable, you should consider transaction log shipping.

Question 2—Do you have a Shared Storage Network (SAN)?

Storage replication should always be the preferred option. Nothing needs to be configured, administered and maintained in the database. Storage replication is fully transparent, has no impact on performance and does not need to be taken into account when doing changes to the database instance. Needless to say, storage replication requires integrated storage. If this is not available, system replication is a valid alternative.

8.3   System Replication versus Storage Replication versus Virtualization

At last, all options in one table. In Table 8.3, we compare the SAP HANA high availability and replication options against the options delivered by virtualization and storage replication. Note that clustering software is needed with SAP HANA system replication and storage replication. The SAP HANA secondary systems are unable to automatically initiate a failover. It always needs to be triggered by the system administrator or automated using cluster software. The same goes for storage replication. A disaster needs to be declared to initiate take-over. Certified storage vendors have tools to do this.

	SAP HANA host failover	SAP HANA system replication	Virtualization	Host restart with storage replication
Scenario	SAP HANA standby host using built-in functionality	Data replication between two SAP HANA systems using built-in functionality	SAP HANA with auto restart and VMware HA	Data replication at storage level
OS Failures	Yes	Yes	Yes	Yes
Hardware Failures	Yes	Yes	Yes	Yes
Application Failures	Yes	Yes	Yes	Yes
Unattended Failover	Yes	No (cluster software)	Yes	No (cluster software)
IP Redirect / DNS update	Not needed	No (cluster software needed)	Not needed	Not needed
RTO	Short	Short	Medium (crash recovery needed)	Long and manual restart
RPO	0	0 (SYNC) >0 (ASYNC)	0	0 (SYNC) >0 (ASYNC)
Performance	Medium, data load	Configurable, short to medium	Medium to long, full SAP HANA restart	Medium to long, full SAP HANA restart
Virtualization supported	Yes	Yes	Yes	Yes

	SAP HANA host failover	SAP HANA system replication	Virtualization	Host restart with storage replication
Standby hardware required	At least 1	Configurable, may be shared with non-production systems	No	Configurable, may be shared with non-production systems
Scale-up supported	Yes	Yes	Yes	Yes
Scale-out supported	Yes	Yes	Yes	Yes
Complexity	Medium	High	Low	High

Table 8.3: Comparison—SAP HANA failover, system replication and virtualization

8.4 Understand your Performance Load!

Performance is important and from an end-user perspective the SAP system is always too slow or too unresponsive. In the world of SAP, performance is related to in-house developments and hardware resources. From a hardware perspective, SAP performance is, in most cases, related to the available memory, number of processors and storage performance. In our experience, the latter is the most important.

How does this impact your system layout? It depends on the solution you implement.

For storage replication and system replication, the secondary needs to be able to keep up with the primary. This is especially the case if you are using system replication with synchronous replication. Synchronous replication implies that the primary database will wait to confirm with the application that the change was successfully written to the database before the secondary database is able to confirm the write as well. The primary and secondary systems need to have the same performance capabilities and the network connection between both needs to have an acceptable latency.

For high availability, what will the performance impact be if the primary cluster node is unavailable? Remember that in clustered SAP environments, application servers are installed on both nodes. Imagine that you have two application servers. You only have one application server left if one of the nodes fails. In numbers, you drop to 50% of your capacity.

What about the data center? If the whole data center fails, do you need to failover to the secondary data center? If these data centers are geographically close together, you can use standard storage replication and high-availability clusters to handle these failovers. If, in addition, your application servers are equally divided among these data centers, you should be able to continue to work. Again, as you lose 50% of your resources, performance will drop.

Figure 8.3 shows an example of a distributed SAP ERP system. Application servers are equally divided among the two data centers. VMware Fault Tolerance protects the single point of failure (SPOF) the ASCS instance (Message and Enqueue server). The database is protected by storage or system replication. In this example, the customer only needs four application servers but has six. As such, performance will drop when the first data center fails, but it will be limited as spare capacity is foreseen in the system setup.

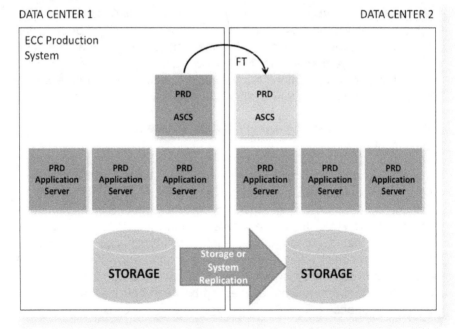

Figure 8.3: Distributed data center layout

9 Appendix: References

Writing a book without preparation and documentation is unwise and creates a recipe for disaster. In writing this book, many existing sources and documentation have been referenced and are listed below.

9.1 SAP Support Notes

SAP Notes and SAP Knowledge Base Articles (KBA) are support documents to help you find answers to questions arising from your daily work with SAP software products.

We referenced the following support notes:

- ▶ 1620213—ERP Accelerators: Enhancement Application Settings
- ▶ 1661202—Support multiple applications one SAP HANA database / tenant DB
- ▶ 1681092—Multiple SAP HANA DBMSs (SIDs) on one SAP HANA system
- ▶ 1694697—SAP Business Application Accelerator powered by HANA
- ▶ 1872170—Suite on HANA—S/4 sizing report
- ▶ 1729988—SAP BW powered by SAP HANA—Checklist Tool
- ▶ 1788665—SAP HANA Support for virtualized / partitioned (multi-tenant) environments
- ▶ 1793345—Sizing for SAP Suite on HANA
- ▶ 1825774—SAP Business Suite Powered by SAP HANA, S/4HANA—Multi-Node Support
- ▶ 1826100—Multiple applications SAP Business Suite powered by SAP HANA
- ▶ 1872170—Suite on HANA—S/4 sizing report
- ▶ 1943937—Hardware Configuration Check Tool—Central Note
- ▶ 1953429—SAP HANA and SAP NetWeaver AS ABAP on one Server

- ▶ 1995460—Single SAP HANA VM on VMware vSphere in production
- ▶ 2024433—Multiple SAP HANA VMs on VMware vSphere in production
- ▶ 2043509—SAP HANA and SAP NetWeaver Java on a Single Host
- ▶ 2055470—HANA on POWER Planning and Installation Specifics - Central Note
- ▶ 2063057—SAP HANA on Hitachi LPAR logical partitions in production
- ▶ 2096000—SAP HANA multitenant database containers— Additional Information
- ▶ 2103848—SAP HANA on HP nPartitions in production
- ▶ 2111714—SAP HANA on Fujitsu PPAR in production
- ▶ 2121768—Considerations with SAP HANA multitenant database containers and SAP BW
- ▶ 2157587—SAP Business Warehouse, powered by SAP HANA on VMware vSphere in scale-out and production
- ▶ 2188482—SAP HANA on IBM Power Systems: Allowed Hardware
- ▶ 2232700—SAP HANA on Lenovo X6 FlexNode in production
- ▶ 2296290—New Sizing Report for BW on HANA
- ▶ 2315348—Single SAP HANA VM on VMware vSphere 6 in production

9.2   Articles and Other Publications

In addition to the SAP support notes, we used the following documentation and white papers:

From SAP:
- ▶ SAP HANA Master Guide
- ▶ SAP HANA Network Requirements
- ▶ SAP HANA Storage Requirements
- ▶ SAP HANA Multitenant Database Containers
- ▶ SAP HANA Tailored Data Center Integration, Frequently Asked Questions

▶ SAP documentation: Sizing Approaches for SAP HANA

▶ How to Perform System Replication for SAP HANA

From VMware:

▶ SAP on VMware Availability and Disaster Recovery Guide

▶ Best Practices and Recommendations for Scale-up Deployments of SAP HANA on VMware vSphere

▶ SAP HANA guidelines for being Virtualized with VMware vSphere

From SUSE:

▶ SAP Applications made high available on SUSE Linux Enterprise Server

▶ SAP HANA System Replication on SLES for SAP Application

From REDHAT:

▶ Automated SAP HANA System Replication with Pacemaker on Red Hat Linux

From IBM:

▶ SAP HANA on IBM Power Systems and IBM Storage

You have finished the book.

A The Author

Bert Vanstechelman

Bert Vanstechelman is partner of and principal technical consultant at Expertum. He has more than 20 years of experience in SAP Basis consulting, covering all kinds of SAP versions in combination with all possible databases and operating systems supported by SAP. Bert specializes in platform migrations, SAP release upgrades and Unicode conversions, and helping customers prepare for the digital Economy. Bert is the founder of Logos Consulting, now part of Expertum.

Bert is a member of the board of advisors of the SAP Professional Journal. He is also the co-author, with Mark Mergaerts, of the following SAP PRESS books: *Upgrading SAP*, *SAP NetWeaver Application Server Upgrade Guide*, *The OS/DB Migration Project Guide* and the *mySAP ERP Upgrade Project Guide*.

You can reach Bert at bert.vanstechelman@expertum.net.

About Expertum

The Expertum team consists entirely of consultants with long and extensive experience in SAP technology.

Expertum offers functional and technical expertise in a broad range of SAP solutions, from S/4HANA, Hybris, Analytics to SAP Security, Solution Manager, ... and the technological know-how on how to best install, migrate, upgrade, integrate, monitor and maintain these SAP solutions and underlying databases.

Our mission is to provide in-depth technical and functional expertise in the SAP area: to assist our customers and our implementation partners during their key projects and daily operations. We aim for long-term relationships in order to assist our customers today and continue to provide them with future-proof strategic platform & solution advice for tomorrow.

Our consultants are our most important assets. We inspire them to be the best and provide them with the necessary support, education and knowledge sharing to do so. This approach provides our customers with focused and motivated individuals who act as trusted advisors.

We strive for continuing relationships in which we guide our customers during periods of high workload. We assist them in large implementation projects, small advisory tracks, roadmaps, proof of concepts,...Remote support, to take the daily administration burden out of our customers' hands, can also be provided.

We strongly believe in the exchange of knowledge and information to the benefit of our consultants and our partners. In co-operation with SAP PRESS, we have published the following SAP books:

- *Upgrading SAP*
- *SAP NetWeaver Application Server Upgrade Guide*
- *ERP Upgrade Project Guide*
- *The SAP OS/DB Migration Project Guide*

Furthermore, we advise the SAP Professional Journal on technical SAP subjects.

Technology Competence Areas

One of our core competence areas is technical consulting for all SAP versions in combination with all databases and operating systems supported by SAP. Our service desk supports customers running DB2, MAXDB, Oracle, SAP HANA, SQL-Server, Sybase and Informix on Windows, AIX, HP-Unix, Linux, Solaris, AS400 and z/OS.

Our areas of expertise include:

- in-memory computing with SAP HANA
- upgrades, enhancement package and support package installations
- OS/DB migrations and Unicode conversions
- installations in high-availability environments
- set-up and design of disaster recovery procedures
- workload analysis, performance and tuning
- system copies and set-up of the Test Data Migration Server (TDMS)
- ABAP Development for Fiori, UI5, Unicode and HANA
- data & document archiving in combination with Open Text
- BI/BO reporting & performance and tuning
- PI/PO implementation
- Enterprise Portal setup and configuration
- Single Sign-on, SAP Security
- Landscape Virtualization Management or SAP LVM

Expertum goes SAP HANA

From 2025, SAP solutions will only be supported on SAP HANA. Several SAP solutions are today already only available on SAP HANA—for example, S/4HANA.

Expertum is the leader in HANA implementation projects in Belgium and the quality and experience of our certified consultants are widely acknowledged. Below are some examples of assignments Expertum has successfully carried out:

- ▶ architectural design for SAP landscapes running on SAP HANA in both appliance and SAP TDI format
- ▶ installations of SAP BW, SAP CRM, S/4HANA and SAP ERP systems running on SAP HANA
- ▶ upgrades and migrations for SAP BW, SAP CRM and SAP ERP from DB2, SQL-Server and Oracle to SAP HANA
- ▶ installation and technical setup of SAP SLT and FICO accelerator on SAP HANA

In line with our strong belief in the exchange of knowledge and information, we have published several white papers and presentations on SAP HANA:

- ▶ *The SAP HANA Released Deployment Options and Migration Methodology.* This presentation was presented at the SAP User Community and Storage & Security Expo in 2014, 2015 and 2016. The presentation is updated regularly to keep up with deployment developments.
- ▶ *The SAP HANA Implementation Guide. Everybody is talking SAP HANA. But what is it really all about and why should I care?* In this book we answer some fundamental questions about SAP HANA, its architecture and deployment options.

About SUSAN

The Susan Smart platform (see Figure A.1) is a comprehensive system for monitoring all aspects of SAP NetWeaver ABAP and SAP NetWeaver Java systems. Susan Smart has been developed by Expertum and builds on the company's extensive expertise in the field of SAP technology.

Expertum uses SAP Solution Manager, which covers a very wide range of SAP solutions, as a foundation for monitoring and supporting customer systems. However, we made the conscious decision that for SAP NetWeaver systems, which are at the very heart of a company's SAP landscape, we needed more than what Solution Manager provides. Leveraging the extensive experience and in-depth knowledge of Expertum consultants has resulted in the unique power and flexibility of Susan Smart.

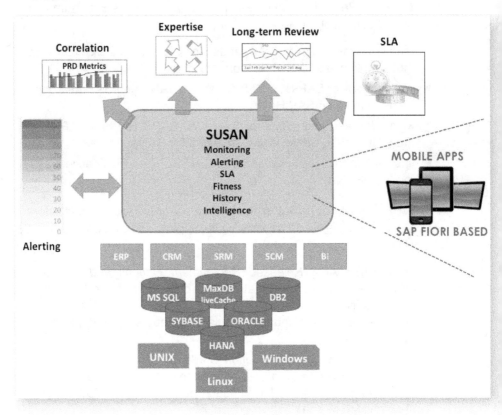

Figure A.1: Susan Smart monitoring, alerting and reporting.

Data Collection and Alerting

Susan Smart monitors the SAP NetWeaver system using a data collection process that is powerful and highly flexible, but has itself a very small footprint. Elements are monitored at (configurable) frequencies that take into account their criticality and their likelihood to change at short notice, with the ability to check crucial KPIs as often as once per minute.

Susan Smart goes beyond the traditional "traffic light" metaphor where a monitored element is simply flagged as green (OK), yellow (warning) or red (problem). Experience shows that this is too crude a method for evaluating the status of a system, especially if, as is the case for the SAP NetWeaver system, the number of monitored elements is large. Instead of the rudimentary red-yellow-green differentiation, Susan Smart uses a sophisticated "color calculus" which takes into account not only the seriousness of the alert but also other things such as the context in which the alert is occurring. This ensures that the status of the system is diagnosed in a fine-grained manner and avoids issues such as "red saturation" where, at any one time, numerous elements are reported with a red status.

Alerts can trigger the automatic creation of a ticket in the support system (Expertum's own support desk is fully integrated with Susan Smart). They can also be configured to trigger other actions such as sending an email or transmitting a text or voice message to an on-call support engineer. Other information channels into which Susan feeds its information are the "kiosk" (the equivalent of the alert inbox in other products), a dashboard showing the status of a system or group of systems at a glance, and a collection of graphs and statistical reports.

Reporting

Monitoring with Susan Smart does more than trigger alerts. The information collected is used to build an extensive knowledge database, which in turn serves as the basis for a set of convenient reports. The collector configuration is so flexible that you can set the frequency of each collector to as low as one minute or as high as days or weeks. This enables you to set up a monitoring schedule that constantly keeps a close eye on the SAP NetWeaver system while at the same time relieving administrators of repetitive work. Here are some examples:

- ▶ The Early Morning Report—System administrators often verify the system every morning through time-consuming and error-prone "transaction hopping", executing transactions such as SM37, SM58, SMQR, SMQS, SM12, SM13, SM50, SM51, SM66, ST22, WE05 and many more. Susan Smart automates this tedious chore by automatically generating its "Early Morning Report", which is ready and waiting for the administrator at the start of the workday. Users can navigate through earlier reports up to 14 days old to examine how an issue has evolved over time.

▶ Hourly reporting—To follow the system status by the hour, Susan Smart generates an hourly update from a full system monitoring report. The hourly updates are then made available in a time-navigable interface. Navigation through earlier reports, up to 48 hours old, is possible.

▶ In the update mode, the hourly reports are continuously updated as new data from the collectors become available, which makes even the reporting facility seem real-time.

▶ High frequency monitoring—Because of Susan Smart's ability to run collectors as often as every minute, it can keep a permanent watch on critical elements of the system. This results in an "immediate response", making any event of interest appear in the kiosk or on the dashboard, generating a support incident and showing up in the reports.

In addition to its monitoring functions, Susan Smart is also capable of generating a detailed system review over any requested time period (weeks, months or even years).

Customization

The design of the Susan collection process makes it very easy to add or enhance data collectors. Our customers have frequently benefited from this capability because we have been able to provide them with alerts within just a few days; with other products this would have taken months or would never have been developed at all due to the specificity of the request. Two real-life examples to illustrate this:

▶ An Expertum customer wanted a specific alert (and the possibility to report) for short dumps that originated in code developed in-house (Z programs). This feature was helpful with a quality review of their internal development.

▶ Another customer wanted a high-level alert and a customized text message if a specific background job did not run or started later than a certain cut-off time. This was a critical job for vehicle planning and thanks to the custom alert the business process could be made more robust.

Installation and Configuration

In contrast with Solution Manager and most third-party monitoring products, Susan Smart is extremely easy to install and maintain. The data collection uses standard functions in SAP as much as possible. Where standard functions are not available, Susan uses a light-weight agent installed in the monitored system; this is the only software to be installed there.

Thanks to its efficient, performance-oriented design, Susan has the capacity to monitor dozens or even hundreds of systems simultaneously. Adding a new system to Susan's watch list can be done in a matter of minutes.

B Index

C Disclaimer

This publication contains references to the products of SAP SE.

SAP, R/3, SAP NetWeaver, Duet, PartnerEdge, ByDesign, SAP BusinessObjects Explorer, StreamWork, and other SAP products and services mentioned herein as well as their respective logos are trademarks or registered trademarks of SAP SE in Germany and other countries.

Business Objects and the Business Objects logo, BusinessObjects, Crystal Reports, Crystal Decisions, Web Intelligence, Xcelsius, and other Business Objects products and services mentioned herein as well as their respective logos are trademarks or registered trademarks of Business Objects Software Ltd. Business Objects is an SAP company.

Sybase and Adaptive Server, iAnywhere, Sybase 365, SQL Anywhere, and other Sybase products and services mentioned herein as well as their respective logos are trademarks or registered trademarks of Sybase, Inc. Sybase is an SAP company.

SAP SE is neither the author nor the publisher of this publication and is not responsible for its content. SAP Group shall not be liable for errors or omissions with respect to the materials. The only warranties for SAP Group products and services are those that are set forth in the express warranty statements accompanying such products and services, if any. Nothing herein should be construed as constituting an additional warranty.

More Espresso Tutorials Books

Rob Frye, Joe Darlak, Dr. Bjarne Berg:

The SAP® BW to HANA Migration Handbook

▶ Proven Techniques for Planning and Executing a Successful Migration

▶ SAP BW on SAP HANA Sizing and Optimization

▶ Building a Solid Migration Business Case

▶ Step-by-Step Runbook for the Migration Process

http://5109.espresso-tutorials.com

Dominique Alfermann, Stefan Hartmann, Benedikt Engel:

SAP® HANA Advanced Modeling

▶ Data modeling guidelines and common test approaches

▶ Modular solutions to complex requirements

▶ Information view performance optimization

▶ Best practices and recommendations

http://4110.espresso-tutorials.com

Janet Salmon & Claus Wild:

First Steps in SAP® S/4HANA Finance

▶ Understand the basics of SAP S/4HANA Finance

▶ Explore the new architecture, configuration options, and SAP Fiori

▶ Examine SAP S/4HANA Finance migration steps

▶ Assess the impact on business processes

http://5149.espresso-tutorials.com

Frank Riesner, Klaus-Peter Sauer:

SAP® BW/4HANA and BW on HANA

▶ Migration, sizing, operation, data management with SAP BW/4HANA and SAP BW 7.5 on HANA

▶ The new central source Systems SAP HANA and ODP

▶ New modeling options, mixed scenarios, LSA++, and differences compared to SAP BW 7.5

▶ The role of BW in operational SAP reporting

http://5215.espresso-tutorials.com

www.ingramcontent.com/pod-product-compliance
Lightning Source LLC
LaVergne TN
LVHW022319060326
832902LV00020B/3565